Common Core Connections
Math

Grade 3

Carson-Dellosa Publishing, LLC
Greensboro, North Carolina

Credits
Content Editor: Marie Shepherd
Copy Editor: Julie B. Killian

 Visit *carsondellosa.com* for correlations to Common Core, state, national, and
Canadian provincial standards.

Carson-Dellosa Publishing, LLC
PO Box 35665
Greensboro, NC 27425 USA
carsondellosa.com

ISBN 978-1-62442-789-3

03-125141151

Table of Contents

Introduction

What are the Common Core State Standards for Mathematics?

The standards are a shared set of expectations for each grade level in the area of math. They define what students should understand and be able to do. The standards are designed to be more rigorous and allow for students to justify their thinking. They reflect the knowledge that is necessary for success in college and beyond.

The following are Standards for Mathematical Practice as outlined in the Common Core State Standards.
1. Make sense of problems and persevere in solving them.
2. Reason abstractly and quantitatively.
3. Construct viable arguments and critique the reasoning of others.
4. Model with mathematics.
5. Use appropriate tools strategically.
6. Attend to precision.
7. Look for and make use of structure.
8. Look for and express regularity in repeated reasoning.*

How to Use This Book

The book is a collection of practice pages aligned to the Common Core State Standards for Mathematics as appropriate for third grade. Included is an alignment matrix so that you can see exactly which standard is addressed on each page. Also included are a skill assessment and skill assessment analysis. The assessment can be used at the beginning of the year or at any time of year you wish to assess your students' mastery of certain standards. The analysis connects each test item to a practice page or set of practice pages so that you can review skills with students who miss certain items.

* © Copyright 2010. National Governors Association Center for Best Practices and Council of Chief State School Officers. All rights reserved.

© Carson-Dellosa • CD-104604

Common Core State Standards*
Alignment Matrix

Pages	3.OA.1	3.OA.2	3.OA.3	3.OA.4	3.OA.5	3.OA.6	3.OA.7	3.OA.8	3.OA.9	3.NBT.1	3.NBT.2	3.NBT.3	3.NF.1	3.NF.2	3.NF.2a	3.NF.2b	3.NF.3	3.NF.3a	3.NF.3b	3.NF.3c	3.NF.3d	3.MD.1	3.MD.2	3.MD.3	3.MD.4	3.MD.5	3.MD.5a	3.MD.5b	3.MD.6	3.MD.7	3.MD.7a	3.MD.7b	3.MD.7c	3.MD.7d	3.MD.8	3.G.1	3.G.2
12	●																																				
13	●																																				
14		●																																			
15		●																																			
16			●																																		
17			●																																		
18			●																																		
19			●																																		
20				●		●																															
21				●					●																												
22	●				●																																
23					●																																
24					●																																
25						●																															
26							●																														
27							●																														
28							●																														
29							●																														
30								●																													
31								●																													
32									●																												
33									●																												
34										●																											
35										●																											
36										●																											
37											●																										
38											●																										
39											●																										
40												●																									
41									●			●																									
42													●																								
43													●																								
44													●																								
45													●																								
46													●																								
47														●	●																						
48														●	●																						
49														●		●																					
50														●		●																					

Common Core State Standards*
Alignment Matrix

Pages	3.OA.1	3.OA.2	3.OA.3	3.OA.4	3.OA.5	3.OA.6	3.OA.7	3.OA.8	3.OA.9	3.NBT.1	3.NBT.2	3.NBT.3	3.NF.1	3.NF.2	3.NF.2a	3.NF.2b	3.NF.3	3.NF.3a	3.NF.3b	3.NF.3c	3.NF.3d	3.MD.1	3.MD.2	3.MD.3	3.MD.4	3.MD.5	3.MD.5a	3.MD.5b	3.MD.6	3.MD.7	3.MD.7a	3.MD.7b	3.MD.7c	3.MD.7d	3.MD.8	3.G.1	3.G.2
51														●	●	●																					
52																	●	●																			
53																	●	●																			
54																	●	●																			
55																	●		●																		
56																	●		●																		
57																	●		●																		
58																	●			●																	
59																	●			●																	
60														●		●	●	●		●																	
61																	●				●																
62																	●				●																
63																						●															
64																						●															
65																						●															
66																						●															
67																						●															
68																						●															
69																						●															
70																						●															
71																							●														
72																							●														
73																								●													
74																								●													
75																								●													
76																									●												
77																									●												
78																									●												
79																										●	●	●	●								
80																										●	●	●	●								
81																														●	●	●					
82																														●			●	●			
83																																			●		
84																														●	●				●		
85																																				●	
86																																				●	
87																																				●	
88																																				●	
89																																					●
90																																					●

Name_____

Solve the problems.

1. ○○ ○○ ○○
   ○○ ○○ ○○

   _____ groups of _____

   _____ × _____ = _____

2. How many 6s are in 24?
   Draw a picture.

3. Cole had 7 bags. He placed 9 strawberries in each bag. How many strawberries did he have?

4. Kim has 24 stickers. She wants to give 6 stickers to each of her friends. How many friends can she give stickers to?

5. A. _____ × 5 = 40

   B. 3 × _____ = 9

   C. _____ ÷ 9 = 5

   D. 20 ÷ 5 = _____

6. A. 3 × 5 = _____ × 3

   B. (2 × 4) × 7 = _____

   C. 24 × 3 = (_____ × 3) + (_____ × 3)

7. Think about 8 × _____ = 32. Use this fact to solve the problem.

   32 ÷ 8 = _____

8. Create a fact family for 3, 5, and 15.

   _____ × _____ = _____

   _____ × _____ = _____

   _____ ÷ _____ = _____

   _____ ÷ _____ = _____

9. Dad bought 17 cookies for a family treat. There are 3 people in the family. How many cookies will each person get? How many will be left over?

10. Highlight the multiples of 2. What pattern do you notice?

×	1	2	3	4	5	6	7	8	9	10	11	12
1	1	2	3	4	5	6	7	8	9	10	11	12
2	2	4	6	8	10	12	14	16	18	20	22	24
3	3	6	9	12	15	18	21	24	27	30	33	36
4	4	8	12	16	20	24	28	32	36	40	44	48

Name_____

Solve the problems.

11. What is 254 rounded to the nearest ten? What is 254 rounded to the nearest hundred?	12. 33 53 +16 −11

13.   47   41
   +14   −15
	14. 230 648
	   +548 −324

15. 828 928 +264 −199	16. $5 \times 10 =$ $5 \times 20 =$ $5 \times 70 =$ $5 \times 90 =$
17. Write the fraction. 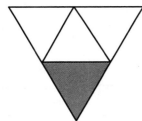 	18. There are 2 blue pens, 4 red pens, and 1 black pen in a backpack. What fraction of the pens are blue?
19. Label the missing fractions. 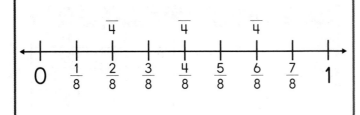	20. Draw a number line. Label it with $\frac{1}{3}$, $\frac{2}{3}$, $\frac{3}{3}$, 0, and 1.

8

Name_____

Solve the problems.

21. Write 2 different ways to name the fraction.

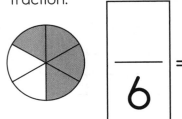

$$\frac{\quad}{6} = \frac{\quad}{3}$$

22. Write 3 fractions that are equivalent to $\frac{1}{2}$.

23. Name the fraction.

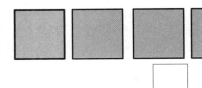

$$5 = \frac{\quad}{1}$$

24. Use >, <, or = to compare the fractions.

25. What time is it?

_____ : _____

9:37

26. Jackie will go to recess at 11:50 am. She will go to lunch at 12:25 pm. How long is recess?

27. Circle the best unit of measure.

A. The amount of water in a large bucket: L mL

B. The mass of a book: g kg

28. How much time was spent on homework in all?

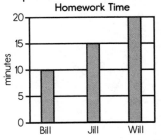

29. How many more people voted for blue than red?

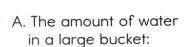

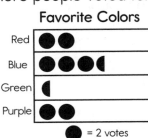

= 2 votes

30. Measure to the nearest quarter inch.

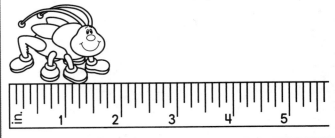

Name_____

Solve the problems.

31. How many people have a shoe size of $5\frac{1}{2}$ or greater?

Shoe Sizes

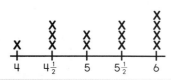

32. Find the area.

A = _____

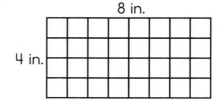

33. Find the area.

A = _____

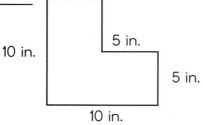

4 in.

34. Use the distributive property to find the area.

A = _____

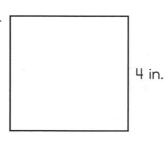

24 in.

4 in.

35. Find the area.

A = _____

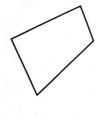

10 in.

5 in.

5 in.

10 in.

36. Find the perimeter.

P = _____

5 cm

2 cm

2 cm

3 cm

1 cm

37. Name the polygon.

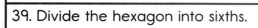

_____   _____

38. Draw a quadrilateral.

39. Divide the hexagon into sixths.

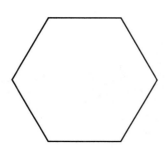

40. Draw a triangle. Shade $\frac{3}{4}$ of it.

10

© Carson-Dellosa • CD-104604

After you review your student's skill assessment, match those problems answered incorrectly to the Common Core State Standards below. Pay special attention to the pages that fall into these problem sections, and ensure that your student receives supervision in these areas. In this way, your student will strengthen these skills.

Answer Key: 1. 3 groups of 4; 3 × 4 = 12; 2. 4, Drawings will vary. 3. 63 strawberries; 4. 4 friends; 5. A. 8 × 5 = 40, B. 3 × 3 = 9, C. 45 ÷ 9 = 5, D. 20 ÷ 5 = 4; 6. A. 3 × 5 = 5 × 3, B. (2 × 4) × 7 = 56, C. Answers will vary. 7. 8 × 4 = 32, 32 ÷ 8 = 4; 8. 3 × 5 = 15, 5 × 3 = 15, 15 ÷ 3 = 5, 15 ÷ 5 = 3; 9. 5 cookies, 2 left over; 10. Answers will vary. 11. 250, 300; 12. 49, 42; 13. 61, 26; 14. 778, 324; 15. 1,092, 729; 16. 50, 100, 350, 450; 17. $\frac{1}{4}$; 18. $\frac{2}{7}$; 19. $\frac{1}{4}$, $\frac{2}{4}$, $\frac{3}{4}$; 20. [number line from 0 to 1 marked $\frac{1}{3}$, $\frac{2}{3}$, $\frac{3}{3}$]; 21. $\frac{4}{6} = \frac{2}{3}$; 22. Answers will vary but may include $\frac{2}{4}$, $\frac{3}{6}$, $\frac{4}{8}$; 23. $\frac{5}{1}$; 24. =; 25. 11:20, Check students' answers. 26. 35 minutes; 27. A. L, B. g; 28. 45 minutes; 29. 3 people; 30. 1 $\frac{3}{4}$ in; 31. 7 people; 32. 32 sq. in; 33. 16 sq. in; 34. 56 sq. in; 35. 75 sq. in; 36. 20 cm; 37. quadrilateral, rhombus; 38. Answers will vary but should include a four-sided figure.

39. [hexagon divided into 6 triangles] ; 40. [triangle divided into 4 triangles with 2 shaded]

Common Core State Standards*		Test Item(s)	Practice Page(s)
Operations and Algebraic Thinking			
Represent and solve problems involving multiplication and division.	3.OA.1–3.OA.4	1–5	12–22
Understand properties of multiplication and the relationship between multiplication and division.	3.OA.5–3.OA.6	6–7	20, 22–25
Multiply and divide within 100.	3.OA.7	8	26–29
Solve problems involving the four operations, and identify and explain patterns in arithmetic.	3.OA.8–3.OA.9	9–10	21, 30–33, 41
Number and Operations in Base Ten			
Use place value understanding and properties of operations to perform multi-digit arithmetic.	3.NBT.1–3.NBT.3	11–16	34–41
Number and Operations—Fractions			
Develop understanding of fractions as numbers.	3.NF.1–3.NF.3	17–24	42–62
Measurement and Data			
Solve problems involving measurement and estimation of intervals of time, liquid volumes, and masses of objects.	3.MD.1–3.MD.2	25–27	63–70
Represent and interpret data.	3.MD.3–3.MD.4	28–31	73–78
Geometric measurement: understand concepts of area and relate area to multiplication and to addition.	3.MD.5–3.MD.7	32–35	79–82, 84
Geometric measurement: recognize perimeter as an attribute of plane figures and distinguish between linear and area measures.	3.MD.8	36	83–84
Geometry			
Reason with shapes and their attributes.	3.G.1–3.G.2	37–40	85–90

Name_____

Draw a line from each multiplication problem to the way to say it. Then, draw a line to the matching picture.

1. 3 × 2 = _____

4 groups of 2

2. 2 × 5 = _____

3 groups of 4

3. 4 × 2 = _____

3 groups of 2

4. 3 × 4 = _____

2 groups of 5

5. 4 × 5 = _____

5 groups of 5

6. 5 × 5 = _____

4 groups of 5

Draw groups of pictures to show each problem.

7. 4 × 4 = _____   8.   3 × 3 = _____

□ I can use multiplication to figure out the total number of objects in an array or equal groups.

12

Write a word problem to match each description. Solve the problem. Draw a picture and write the equation.

1. 7 groups of 3

_____
_____
_____
_____
_____

2. 6 groups of 5

_____
_____
_____
_____
_____

3. 4 groups of 9

_____
_____
_____
_____
_____

4. 12 groups of 6

_____
_____
_____
_____

☐ I can use multiplication to figure out the total number of objects in an array or equal groups.

Solve each problem.

Example: 20 ÷ 4   How many 4s are in 20? __5__
Draw a picture: Subtract down:

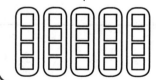

20 – 4 = __16__   16 – 4 = __12__   12 – 4 = __8__
8 – 4 = __4__   4 – 4 = __0__

1. 21 ÷ 3
   How many 3s are in 21? _____

   Draw a picture. Subtract down.

2. 30 ÷ 5
   How many 5s are in 30? _____

   Draw a picture. Subtract down.

3. 36 ÷ 9
   How many 9s are in 36? _____

   Draw a picture. Subtract down.

4. 18 ÷ 6
   How many 6s are in 18? _____

   Draw a picture. Subtract down.

☐ I can divide to show how to share a set of objects equally.
☐ I can use division to divide a set of objects into equal groups.

Name_____

Write a word problem to match each description. Solve the problem. Draw a picture and write the equation.

1. 21 divided into 7 groups

_____
_____
_____
_____
_____

2. 45 divided into 5 groups

_____
_____
_____
_____
_____

3. 36 divided into 6 groups

_____
_____
_____
_____
_____

4. 18 divided into 2 groups

_____
_____
_____
_____
_____

☐ I can divide to show how to share a set of objects equally.
☐ I can use division to divide a set of objects into equal groups.

Name_____

Solve each problem. Draw a picture in the box to help you. Write your answer on the line.

1. Randy had 6 bags. He placed 9 marbles in each bag. How many marbles did he have?

_____

2. Taron has 4 stacks of cards with 8 cards in each stack. How many cards does he have?

_____

3. Jennifer jumped over 5 rocks. She jumped over each rock 9 times. How many times did she jump?

_____

4. Zach runs 6 miles, 5 days a week. How many miles does he run in a week?

_____

5. The skaters skated in 7 groups with 4 in each group. How many skaters were present in all of the groups?

_____

6. Eight children went for a hike. Each child carried a backpack with 6 bandages in it. How many total bandages did they have?

_____

☐ I can multiply to solve word problems.

16

Draw an array to help you solve a multiplication problem. Then, count the number of marks you made.

$3 \times 5 =$ ___15___

Solve each problem. Draw an array in the box to help you. Write your answer on the line.

1. The store display had 9 shelves. The stock boy placed 9 boxes of cereal on each shelf. How many boxes of cereal were on display?

_____

2. The third graders formed 8 relay teams. Seven students were on each team. How many students were running the relay?

_____

3. Ms. Martinez made a scrapbook for her daughter. The scrapbook had 7 pages. Each page had 6 pictures. How many pictures were in the scrapbook?

_____

4. John keeps his baseball cards in a notebook. His notebook has 8 pages. Each page has 9 cards. How many cards does John have?

_____

5. Jenna wrote 2 pages in her diary each day of the week. How many pages did she write each week?

_____

6. Carlos has 5 jars of marbles. He has 8 marbles in each jar. How many marbles does he have?

_____

☐ I can multiply to solve word problems.

Solve each problem. Draw a picture in the box to help you. Write your answer on the line.

1. David has 12 goldfish. He has 2 fish tanks. How many goldfish will be in each tank if he divides them evenly?

_____

2. Daysha bought 8 bracelets. She will wear the same number on each wrist. How many bracelets will she have on each wrist?

_____

3. Sam's team scored 16 points. They scored the same number of points in each of the 4 quarters. How many points did they score in each quarter?

_____

4. Rashad has 15 trophies. He displays them evenly on 3 shelves. How many trophies are on each shelf?

_____

5. Jan has 18 buttons. She has 6 pockets on her pants. She sewed the same number of buttons on each pocket. How many buttons did she sew on each pocket?

_____

6. Keisha has 35 new photos to add to her album. She will place 5 photos on each page. How many pages will she need?

_____

☐ I can divide to solve word problems.

Solve each problem. Draw a picture in the box to help you. Write your answer on the line.

1. Ben has 72 stamps. He has 8 pages in his stamp book. If he places the same number of stamps on each page, how many stamps will be on each page?

_____

2. Jared found 56 rocks for his collection. He divided the rocks into 7 equal groups. How many rocks did he have in each group?

_____

3. Meisha had 81 beads to make necklaces. She used 9 beads for each necklace. How many necklaces did she make?

_____

4. Simone runs 21 miles each week. She runs the same distance every day. How many miles does she run each day?

_____

5. Mikayla has 42 crayons. She has 6 bins. She wants to keep the same number of crayons in each bin. How many crayons will she keep in each bin?

_____

6. Nick needs to read 45 minutes each week. He reads for the same amount of time Monday through Friday. How many minutes does he read each day?

_____

☐ I can divide to solve word problems.

Name_____

Find each missing number.

1. $3 \times$ _____ $= 27$ $7 \times$ _____ $= 42$ $5 \times$ _____ $= 50$ $12 \times$ _____ $= 36$

2. _____ $\times 7 = 49$ $9 \times$ _____ $= 81$ $4 \times$ _____ $= 28$ _____ $\times 8 = 32$

3. _____ $\times 5 = 45$ _____ $\times 4 = 12$ _____ $\times 8 = 72$ $6 \times$ _____ $= 24$

4. _____ $\times 8 = 64$ $6 \times$ _____ $= 48$ _____ $\times 7 = 63$ $10 \times$ _____ $= 100$

5. $6 \times$ _____ $= 42$ _____ $\times 4 = 16$ $8 \times$ _____ $= 40$ _____ $\times 3 = 21$

Find each missing number. Use a multiplication fact to help you.

6. $48 \div \boxed{} = 8$ $36 \div \boxed{} = 6$ $36 \div \boxed{} = 4$

7. $\boxed{} \div 7 = 6$ $\boxed{} \div 9 = 5$ $\boxed{} \div 4 = 7$

8. $\boxed{} \div 10 = 8$ $63 \div \boxed{} = 9$ $27 \div \boxed{} = 3$

9. $5 = 15 \div \boxed{}$ $6 = \boxed{} \div 5$ $10 = \boxed{} \div 3$

10. $22 = 44 \div \boxed{}$ $7 = \boxed{} \div 7$ $7 = 56 \div \boxed{}$

☐ I can find a missing number in a multiplication or division problem.
☐ I can use my understanding of multiplication to solve division problems.

Look at each pattern. Complete the chart.

1.

Rule: × 2	
2	4
3	6
4	8
5	10
6	
7	
8	

2.

Rule: ÷ 3	
12	4
21	7
30	10
15	
60	
24	
9	

3.

Rule: × 5	
2	10
3	15
4	20
5	
6	
7	
8	

4.

Rule: ÷ 4	
40	10
32	8
4	1
44	
36	
28	
16	

5.

Rule:	
2	8
3	12
4	16
5	20
6	24
7	28
8	32

6.

Rule:	
20	4
35	7
40	8
15	3
5	1
10	2
50	10

☐ I can find a missing number in a multiplication or division problem.
☐ I can identify and explain patterns.

Use the pictures to represent each problem. Solve the problem.

Example: 2 × 3 = 6, 3 × 2 = 6

1. _____ × _____ = _____   _____ × _____ = _____

2. _____ × _____ = _____   _____ × _____ = _____

3. _____ × _____ = _____   _____ × _____ = _____

4. _____ × _____ = _____   _____ × _____ = _____

5. _____ × _____ = _____   _____ × _____ = _____

6. _____ × _____ = _____   _____ × _____ = _____

Draw a picture to match each problem. Solve the problem.

7. 6 × 4 = _____   8. 5 × 6 = _____

9. 2 × 7 = _____   10. 8 × 2 = _____

11. 3 × 8 = _____   12. 2 × 9 = _____

Complete each equation.

13. 8 × 3 = 3 × ___8___   14. 5 × 4 = 4 × _____

15. 7 × 2 = _____ × 7   16. 4 × 3 = _____ × 4

17. 3 × 6 = 6 × _____   18. 2 × 9 = _____ × 2

☐ I can use multiplication to figure out the total number of objects in an array or equal groups.
☐ I can use my understanding of multiplication to solve division problems.

3.OA.5

Use the associative property to solve each problem in two different ways.

> **Example**
> $3 \times 5 \times 2$ $(3 \times 5) \times 2 =$ $3 \times (5 \times 2) =$
> $15 \times 2 = 30$ $3 \times 10 = 30$

1. $2 \times 6 \times 1 =$	2. $9 \times 10 \times 1 =$
3. $7 \times 4 \times 3 =$	4. $8 \times 3 \times 2 =$
5. $10 \times 5 \times 4 =$	6. $3 \times 4 \times 2 =$
7. $4 \times 2 \times 5 =$	8. $2 \times 10 \times 3 =$

☐ **I can use properties of multiplication and division to solve problems.**

> The distributive property can multiplying large numbers easier.
>
> 8 × 15 = ?   Think: How can I make this factor smaller?
> 8 × (10 + 5)
> (8 × 10) + (8 × 5)
> 80 + 40 = 120

Use the distributive property to solve each problem.

1. 7 x 8 = ☐

 7 × (_____ + _____)

 (7 × _____) + (7 × _____)

 _____ + _____ =

2. 3 × 17 = ☐

 3 × (_____ + _____)

 (3 × _____) + (3 × _____)

 _____ + _____ =

3. 22 × 5 = ☐

4. 4 × 18 = ☐

5. 6 × 13 = ☐

6. 7 × 12 = ☐

☐ **I can use properties of multiplication and division to solve problems.**

A **dividend** is the number being divided. A **divisor** is the number by which the dividend is divided. A **quotient** is the answer to a division problem.

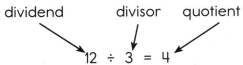

dividend   divisor   quotient

$12 \div 3 = 4$

divisor $\dfrac{4}{3)\overline{12}}$ ← quotient

dividend

Knowing how to multiply can help you divide. Ask yourself: What number multiplied by the divisor equals the dividend? 3 x _____ = 12   3 x 4 = 12

Divide. Write the multiplication fact that helped you. Then, match the quotients to the numbers below and fill in the correct letters.

W	T	I	F
1. $7)\overline{42}$	2. $9)\overline{9}$	3. $6)\overline{30}$	4. $5)\overline{40}$
A	**S**	**L**	**R**
5. $8)\overline{56}$	6. $3)\overline{27}$	7. $8)\overline{80}$	8. $8)\overline{16}$
	K	**E**	
	9. $9)\overline{36}$	10. $7)\overline{21}$	

The first bicycles had no pedals. People walked them along until they came to a hill. Then, they rode down the hill.

What was the first bicycle called?

___ ___ ___ ___ ___ ___ ___ ___ ___ ___ ___ ___
7   9   6   5   8   1   6   7   10   4   3   2

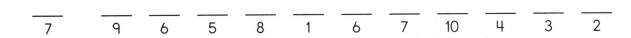

☐ **I can use my understanding of multiplication to solve division problems.**

Name_____

3.OA.7

Solve each problem.

1. $6 \times 5 =$ _____ $7 \times 7 =$ _____ $9 \times 3 =$ _____ $4 \times 8 =$ _____

2. $5 \times 9 =$ _____ $6 \times 3 =$ _____ $7 \times 6 =$ _____ $9 \times 5 =$ _____

3. $9 \times 9 =$ _____ $8 \times 3 =$ _____ $3 \times 7 =$ _____ $4 \times 9 =$ _____

4. $8 \times 7 =$ _____ $9 \times 6 =$ _____ $6 \times 6 =$ _____ $8 \times 8 =$ _____

5.
$$\begin{array}{r} 2 \\ \times 4 \\ \hline \end{array} \quad \begin{array}{r} 10 \\ \times 6 \\ \hline \end{array} \quad \begin{array}{r} 5 \\ \times 3 \\ \hline \end{array} \quad \begin{array}{r} 3 \\ \times 6 \\ \hline \end{array} \quad \begin{array}{r} 11 \\ \times 5 \\ \hline \end{array} \quad \begin{array}{r} 4 \\ \times 7 \\ \hline \end{array} \quad \begin{array}{r} 6 \\ \times 4 \\ \hline \end{array}$$

6.
$$\begin{array}{r} 2 \\ \times 3 \\ \hline \end{array} \quad \begin{array}{r} 7 \\ \times 5 \\ \hline \end{array} \quad \begin{array}{r} 2 \\ \times 9 \\ \hline \end{array} \quad \begin{array}{r} 3 \\ \times 8 \\ \hline \end{array} \quad \begin{array}{r} 8 \\ \times 4 \\ \hline \end{array} \quad \begin{array}{r} 2 \\ \times 5 \\ \hline \end{array} \quad \begin{array}{r} 9 \\ \times 3 \\ \hline \end{array}$$

7.
$$\begin{array}{r} 4 \\ \times 4 \\ \hline \end{array} \quad \begin{array}{r} 3 \\ \times 3 \\ \hline \end{array} \quad \begin{array}{r} 9 \\ \times 5 \\ \hline \end{array} \quad \begin{array}{r} 3 \\ \times 4 \\ \hline \end{array} \quad \begin{array}{r} 7 \\ \times 6 \\ \hline \end{array} \quad \begin{array}{r} 5 \\ \times 6 \\ \hline \end{array} \quad \begin{array}{r} 6 \\ \times 8 \\ \hline \end{array}$$

8.
$$\begin{array}{r} 6 \\ \times 6 \\ \hline \end{array} \quad \begin{array}{r} 9 \\ \times 7 \\ \hline \end{array} \quad \begin{array}{r} 8 \\ \times 7 \\ \hline \end{array} \quad \begin{array}{r} 8 \\ \times 5 \\ \hline \end{array} \quad \begin{array}{r} 4 \\ \times 9 \\ \hline \end{array} \quad \begin{array}{r} 4 \\ \times 8 \\ \hline \end{array} \quad \begin{array}{r} 7 \\ \times 7 \\ \hline \end{array}$$

9. $5 \times 5 =$ _____ $4 \times 7 =$ _____ $8 \times 9 =$ _____ $2 \times 7 =$ _____

10. $3 \times 7 =$ _____ $6 \times 9 =$ _____ $10 \times 7 =$ _____ $6 \times 6 =$ _____

☐ I can multiply and divide within 100.

Name_____

Solve each problem. Draw a picture if it helps you find the answer.

Example:

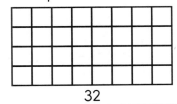 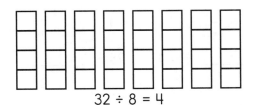 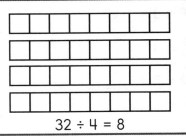

32   32 ÷ 8 = 4   32 ÷ 4 = 8

1. 6 ÷ 2 = _____

6 ÷ 3 = _____

2. 12 ÷ 3 = _____

12 ÷ 4 = _____

3. 15 ÷ 5 = _____

15 ÷ 3 = _____

4. 10 ÷ 5 = _____

10 ÷ 2 = _____

5. 16 ÷ 2 = _____

16 ÷ 8 = _____

6. 20 ÷ 4 = _____

20 ÷ 5 = _____

7. 24 ÷ 6 = _____

24 ÷ 4 = _____

8. 28 ÷ 4 = _____

28 ÷ 7 = _____

9. 36 ÷ 9 = _____

36 ÷ 4 = _____

10. 16 ÷ 8 = _____

16 ÷ 2 = _____

11. 48 ÷ 6 = _____

48 ÷ 8 = _____

12. 54 ÷ 9 = _____

54 ÷ 6 = _____

Shown below is another way to write division problems. Solve each problem.

13. $5\overline{)40}$

14. $6\overline{)42}$

15. $3\overline{)27}$

16. $2\overline{)16}$

17. $7\overline{)49}$

18. $8\overline{)56}$

19. $4\overline{)16}$

20. $9\overline{)45}$

21. $10\overline{)90}$

22. $6\overline{)48}$

23. $7\overline{)56}$

24. $9\overline{)36}$

Write two division problems.

25. _____ ÷ _____ = _____   _____ ÷ _____ = _____

☐ I can multiply and divide within 100.

Solve each problem.

1. $9 \times 3 = \underline{\ 27\ }$ $3 \times 9 = \underline{\hspace{1cm}}$ $27 \div 9 = \underline{\hspace{1cm}}$ $27 \div 3 = \underline{\hspace{1cm}}$

2. $4 \times 7 = \underline{\hspace{1cm}}$ $7 \times 4 = \underline{\hspace{1cm}}$ $28 \div 7 = \underline{\hspace{1cm}}$ $28 \div 4 = \underline{\hspace{1cm}}$

3. $2 \times 8 = \underline{\hspace{1cm}}$ $8 \times 2 = \underline{\hspace{1cm}}$ $16 \div 8 = \underline{\hspace{1cm}}$ $16 \div 2 = \underline{\hspace{1cm}}$

4. $5 \times 6 = \underline{\hspace{1cm}}$ $6 \times 5 = \underline{\hspace{1cm}}$ $30 \div 6 = \underline{\hspace{1cm}}$ $30 \div 5 = \underline{\hspace{1cm}}$

5. $6 \times 9 = \underline{\hspace{1cm}}$ $9 \times 6 = \underline{\hspace{1cm}}$ $54 \div 9 = \underline{\hspace{1cm}}$ $54 \div 6 = \underline{\hspace{1cm}}$

6. $8 \times 7 = \underline{\hspace{1cm}}$ $7 \times 8 = \underline{\hspace{1cm}}$ $56 \div 7 = \underline{\hspace{1cm}}$ $56 \div 8 = \underline{\hspace{1cm}}$

Solve each problem. Then, draw lines to connect the problems that match.

7. $7\overline{)28}$ with 4 above   A. $6 \times 8 = \underline{\hspace{1cm}}$ 13. $5\overline{)40}$ A. $7 \times 8 = \underline{\hspace{1cm}}$

8. $8\overline{)48}$ B. $4 \times 7 = \underline{\ 28\ }$ 14. $8\overline{)56}$ B. $9 \times 7 = \underline{\hspace{1cm}}$

9. $6\overline{)54}$ C. $8 \times 4 = \underline{\hspace{1cm}}$ 15. $4\overline{)24}$ C. $8 \times 5 = \underline{\hspace{1cm}}$

10. $5\overline{)35}$ D. $9 \times 6 = \underline{\hspace{1cm}}$ 16. $7\overline{)63}$ D. $6 \times 4 = \underline{\hspace{1cm}}$

11. $9\overline{)72}$ E. $7 \times 5 = \underline{\hspace{1cm}}$ 17. $6\overline{)42}$ E. $3 \times 9 = \underline{\hspace{1cm}}$

12. $4\overline{)32}$ F. $8 \times 9 = \underline{\hspace{1cm}}$ 18. $9\overline{)27}$ F. $7 \times 6 = \underline{\hspace{1cm}}$

☐ I can multiply and divide within 100.

Use the numbers in each fact family to create different equations.

1.

___7___ × ___8___ = ___56___

___8___ × ___7___ = ___56___

___56___ ÷ ___8___ = ___7___

___56___ ÷ ___7___ = ___8___

2.

_____ × _____ = _____

_____ × _____ = _____

_____ ÷ _____ = _____

_____ ÷ _____ = _____

3.

_____ × _____ = _____

_____ × _____ = _____

_____ ÷ _____ = _____

_____ ÷ _____ = _____

4.

_____ × _____ = _____

_____ × _____ = _____

_____ ÷ _____ = _____

_____ ÷ _____ = _____

5.

_____ × _____ = _____

_____ × _____ = _____

_____ ÷ _____ = _____

_____ ÷ _____ = _____

6.

_____ × _____ = _____

_____ × _____ = _____

_____ ÷ _____ = _____

_____ ÷ _____ = _____

7.

_____ × _____ = _____

_____ × _____ = _____

_____ ÷ _____ = _____

_____ ÷ _____ = _____

8.

_____ × _____ = _____

_____ × _____ = _____

_____ ÷ _____ = _____

_____ ÷ _____ = _____

9.

_____ × _____ = _____

_____ × _____ = _____

_____ ÷ _____ = _____

_____ ÷ _____ = _____

10.

_____ × _____ = _____

_____ ÷ _____ = _____

11.

8 8
64

_____ × _____ = _____

_____ ÷ _____ = _____

12.

9 9
81

_____ × _____ = _____

_____ ÷ _____ = _____

☐ I can multiply and divide within 100.

Use the table to answer each question.

Sam's Market

Fruit	Price
cherries	$2.99 per lb.
apples	$0.89 per lb.
grapes	$1.49 per lb.
strawberries	$3.49 per basket
bananas	$0.59 per lb.
pineapples	$1.99 each

1. Jose wants to buy 1 pound of grapes and 1 pineapple. He has $5.00. Can he purchase these two items? Explain.

_____

_____

2. Jeremy needs 1 basket of strawberries, 1 pineapple, and 1 pound of cherries to make a fruit salad. If he pays with a $10.00 bill, will he get change back? Explain.

_____

_____

3. Andy has 6 quarters. Does he have enough money to buy 1 pineapple? Explain.

_____

_____

4. Anna had $10.00. She bought 3 pounds of fruit. She got $5.53 in change. What fruit did she buy? Explain.

_____

_____

☐ I can use the four operations to solve two-step word problems where a variable is used to represent an unknown quantity.
☐ I can use strategies to decide if my answer is reasonable.

Solve each problem.

1. Kristin made half as many sundaes as Reese. If they made 30 sundaes in all, how many did Kristin make?

_____

2. Chang has 36 dog bones. He has 5 dogs. If he buys 4 more bones, how many bones will each dog get?

_____

3. Alex has 11 apples. He needs 5 apples to make 1 pie. If he has to make 5 pies, how many more apples does he need?

_____

4. Upton and Nassim were playing basketball. Upton won twice as many times as he lost. He won 14 games. How many games did the boys play?

_____

5. Jenny has 19 walnuts. She wants to divide them evenly into 4 bags. If she eats 3 walnuts, how many will she put into each bag?

_____

6. Mom bought 15 cookies for dessert. There are 4 people in the family. How many cookies will each person get? How many will be left over?

_____

☐ I can use the four operations to solve two-step word problems where a variable is used to represent an unknown quantity.
☐ I can use strategies to decide if my answer is reasonable.

Numbers frequently create patterns. Use markers or crayons to identify different number patterns on the addition charts. Show more than one pattern on each chart, using a different color for each. Explain your patterns.

Example:

+	0	1	2	3	4	5	6	7	8	9	10
0	0	1	2	3	4	5	6	7	8	9	10
1	1	2	3	4	5	6	7	8	9	10	11
2	2	3	4	5	6	7	8	9	10	11	12
3	3	4	5	6	7	8	9	10	11	12	13
4	4	5	6	7	8	9	10	11	12	13	14
5	5	6	7	8	9	10	11	12	13	14	15
6	6	7	8	9	10	11	12	13	14	15	16
7	7	8	9	10	11	12	13	14	15	16	17
8	8	9	10	11	12	13	14	15	16	17	18
9	9	10	11	12	13	14	15	16	17	18	19
10	10	11	12	13	14	15	16	17	18	19	20

increases by 1 each time _____

_____

_____

_____

_____

+	0	1	2	3	4	5	6	7	8	9	10
0	0	1	2	3	4	5	6	7	8	9	10
1	1	2	3	4	5	6	7	8	9	10	11
2	2	3	4	5	6	7	8	9	10	11	12
3	3	4	5	6	7	8	9	10	11	12	13
4	4	5	6	7	8	9	10	11	12	13	14
5	5	6	7	8	9	10	11	12	13	14	15
6	6	7	8	9	10	11	12	13	14	15	16
7	7	8	9	10	11	12	13	14	15	16	17
8	8	9	10	11	12	13	14	15	16	17	18
9	9	10	11	12	13	14	15	16	17	18	19
10	10	11	12	13	14	15	16	17	18	19	20

_____

_____

_____

_____

_____

☐ I can identify and explain patterns.

Name_____

Complete the chart. Then, answer each question.

×	1	2	3	4	5	6	7	8	9
1									
2									
3									
4									
5									
6									
7									
8									
9									

1. What does any number times 1 equal? _____

2. What pattern do you see in the 2s? _____

3. What pattern do you see in the 5s? _____

4. Add the digits for each answer in the 9s. What do they each equal? _____

5. 3 × 4 = 12. What does 4 × 3 equal? _____

☐ I can identify and explain patterns.

Name_____

When rounding to the nearest ten, follow these steps:
  1. Look at the ones place.
  2. If the digit is 0, 1, 2, 3, or 4, round down.
  3. If the digit is 5, 6, 7, 8, or 9, round up.

Examples: 3<u>4</u> rounds down to 30.
                3<u>7</u> rounds up to 40.

Round to the nearest ten.

1. 39 _____

2. 62 _____

3. 55 _____

4. 93 _____

5. 74 _____

6. 33 _____

7. 26 _____

8. 41 _____

9. 24 _____

10. 38 _____

11. 296 _____

12. 989 _____

13. 458 _____

14. 434 _____

15. 692 _____

16. 916 _____

17. 776 _____

18. 381 _____

19. 252 _____

20. 722 _____

21. Mariah ate 21 almonds and 17 peanuts. About how many nuts did she eat in all?

22. Meg had 97 stamps. Tony had 83 stamps. About how many more stamps did Meg have than Tony?

_____

_____

☐ I can round a whole number to the nearest 10 and nearest 100.

When rounding to the nearest hundred, follow these steps:
 1. Look at the tens place.
 2. If the digit is 1, 2, 3, or 4, round down.
 3. If the digit is 5, 6, 7, 8, or 9, round up.

Examples: 7<u>4</u>4 rounds down to 700.
          7<u>8</u>2 rounds up to 800.

Round the amount in each treasure chest to the nearest hundred.

1.
$692
$ _____

2.
$140
$ _____

3.
$569
$ _____

4.
$303
$ _____

5.
$684
$ _____

6.
$851
$ _____

7.
$712
$ _____

8.
$476
$ _____

9.
$925
$ _____

☐ I can round a whole number to the nearest 10 and nearest 100.

Round to the nearest ten.

1. 72 _____   2. 55 _____   3. 14 _____   4. 62 _____

5. 83 _____   6. 17 _____   7. 49 _____   8. 29 _____

Round to the nearest hundred.

9. 284 _____   10. 924 _____   11. 561 _____   12. 354 _____

13. 752 _____   14. 728 _____   15. 689 _____   16. 192 _____

17. Sam's basketball team scored 42 points. Nick's team scored 28 points. About how many more points did Sam's team score than Nick's?

_____

18. Janelle had 57 seashells. Her aunt sent her 26 more seashells for her collection. About how many seashells does Jan have now?

_____

19. Roberto had 346 trading cards. He sold 188 cards at a trading show. About how many cards does he have left?

_____

20. Malia's class saved 121 soup labels. The rest of the school saved 699 labels. About how many labels does the school have in all?

_____

☐ I can round a whole number to the nearest 10 and nearest 100.

Name_____

Use the numbers in each fact family to create different equations.

1.

_____ + _____ = _____
_____ + _____ = _____
_____ - _____ = _____
_____ - _____ = _____

2.

8 15
7

_____ + _____ = _____
_____ + _____ = _____
_____ - _____ = _____
_____ - _____ = _____

3.

_____ + _____ = _____
_____ + _____ = _____
_____ - _____ = _____
_____ - _____ = _____

4.

_____ + _____ = _____
_____ + _____ = _____
_____ - _____ = _____
_____ - _____ = _____

5.

16 7
9

_____ + _____ = _____
_____ + _____ = _____
_____ - _____ = _____
_____ - _____ = _____

6.

6 7
13

_____ + _____ = _____
_____ + _____ = _____
_____ - _____ = _____
_____ - _____ = _____

7.

43 23
66

_____ + _____ = _____
_____ + _____ = _____
_____ - _____ = _____
_____ - _____ = _____

8.

52 33
85

_____ + _____ = _____
_____ + _____ = _____
_____ - _____ = _____
_____ - _____ = _____

9.

71 39
110

_____ + _____ = _____
_____ + _____ = _____
_____ - _____ = _____
_____ - _____ = _____

Create three fact families of your choice.

10. _____ + _____ = _____
_____ + _____ = _____
_____ - _____ = _____
_____ - _____ = _____

11. _____ + _____ = _____
_____ + _____ = _____
_____ - _____ = _____
_____ - _____ = _____

12. _____ + _____ = _____
_____ + _____ = _____
_____ - _____ = _____
_____ - _____ = _____

13. Find the missing number.

$8 +$ ☐ $= 14$ $14 -$ ☐ $= 8$ $14 - 8 =$ ☐   ☐ $+ 8 = 14$

☐ I can use strategies for adding and subtracting within 1,000.

Name_____

Solve each problem.

1.   34   28   81   54   84   17
    +15   + 31   + 17   + 35   + 12   + 32

2.   51   73   14   20   41   36
    + 22   + 14   + 13   + 48   + 54   + 21

3.   86   52   67   95   87   48
    −32   −12   −45   −30   −26   −33

4.   39   66   38   75   88   74
    −13   −46   −14   −52   −37   −24

5.   182   231   825   436   325
    +703   + 547   + 163   + 562   + 202

6.   274   641   908   365   207
    + 320   + 345   + 61   +424   + 712

7.   684   634   835   738   325
    −253   −421   −610   −502   − 102

8.   874   647   958   363   567
    − 321   −325   − 146   −242   −362

☐ I can use strategies when adding and subtracting within 1,000.

Solve each problem by regrouping.

1.
$$\begin{array}{r} 27 \\ + 24 \\ \hline \end{array}$$
$$\begin{array}{r} 39 \\ + 53 \\ \hline \end{array}$$
$$\begin{array}{r} 46 \\ + 35 \\ \hline \end{array}$$
$$\begin{array}{r} 57 \\ + 29 \\ \hline \end{array}$$
$$\begin{array}{r} 49 \\ + 15 \\ \hline \end{array}$$
$$\begin{array}{r} 63 \\ + 27 \\ \hline \end{array}$$

2.
$$\begin{array}{r} 75 \\ + 19 \\ \hline \end{array}$$
$$\begin{array}{r} 93 \\ + 37 \\ \hline \end{array}$$
$$\begin{array}{r} 58 \\ + 34 \\ \hline \end{array}$$
$$\begin{array}{r} 64 \\ + 28 \\ \hline \end{array}$$
$$\begin{array}{r} 86 \\ + 17 \\ \hline \end{array}$$
$$\begin{array}{r} 74 \\ + 28 \\ \hline \end{array}$$

3.
$$\begin{array}{r} 36 \\ - 17 \\ \hline \end{array}$$
$$\begin{array}{r} 98 \\ - 19 \\ \hline \end{array}$$
$$\begin{array}{r} 28 \\ - 9 \\ \hline \end{array}$$
$$\begin{array}{r} 41 \\ - 15 \\ \hline \end{array}$$
$$\begin{array}{r} 33 \\ - 17 \\ \hline \end{array}$$
$$\begin{array}{r} 67 \\ - 18 \\ \hline \end{array}$$

4.
$$\begin{array}{r} 72 \\ - 53 \\ \hline \end{array}$$
$$\begin{array}{r} 85 \\ - 27 \\ \hline \end{array}$$
$$\begin{array}{r} 43 \\ - 29 \\ \hline \end{array}$$
$$\begin{array}{r} 96 \\ - 37 \\ \hline \end{array}$$
$$\begin{array}{r} 64 \\ - 36 \\ \hline \end{array}$$
$$\begin{array}{r} 50 \\ - 18 \\ \hline \end{array}$$

5.
$$\begin{array}{r} 187 \\ + 753 \\ \hline \end{array}$$
$$\begin{array}{r} 263 \\ + 347 \\ \hline \end{array}$$
$$\begin{array}{r} 827 \\ + 264 \\ \hline \end{array}$$
$$\begin{array}{r} 726 \\ + 585 \\ \hline \end{array}$$
$$\begin{array}{r} 126 \\ + 294 \\ \hline \end{array}$$

6.
$$\begin{array}{r} 283 \\ + 328 \\ \hline \end{array}$$
$$\begin{array}{r} 268 \\ + 345 \\ \hline \end{array}$$
$$\begin{array}{r} 418 \\ + 199 \\ \hline \end{array}$$
$$\begin{array}{r} 385 \\ + 826 \\ \hline \end{array}$$
$$\begin{array}{r} 294 \\ + 765 \\ \hline \end{array}$$

7.
$$\begin{array}{r} 837 \\ - 138 \\ \hline \end{array}$$
$$\begin{array}{r} 516 \\ - 247 \\ \hline \end{array}$$
$$\begin{array}{r} 825 \\ - 356 \\ \hline \end{array}$$
$$\begin{array}{r} 713 \\ - 284 \\ \hline \end{array}$$
$$\begin{array}{r} 624 \\ - 367 \\ \hline \end{array}$$

8.
$$\begin{array}{r} 283 \\ - 96 \\ \hline \end{array}$$
$$\begin{array}{r} 567 \\ - 275 \\ \hline \end{array}$$
$$\begin{array}{r} 928 \\ - 189 \\ \hline \end{array}$$
$$\begin{array}{r} 785 \\ - 496 \\ \hline \end{array}$$
$$\begin{array}{r} 497 \\ - 269 \\ \hline \end{array}$$

☐ I can use strategies when adding and subtracting within 1,000.

Name_____

Look for a pattern to help multiply numbers by 10.
Any whole number times 10 is that number with a 0 added at the end.
Finding the pattern helps you do these in your head.

$$\begin{array}{r} 10 \\ \times\ 2 \\ \hline \mathbf{20} \end{array} \qquad \begin{array}{r} 10 \\ \times\ 3 \\ \hline \mathbf{30} \end{array}$$

Solve each problem.

1.
$$\begin{array}{r} 10 \\ \times\ 8 \\ \hline \end{array} \qquad \begin{array}{r} 10 \\ \times\ 7 \\ \hline \end{array} \qquad \begin{array}{r} 10 \\ \times\ 4 \\ \hline \end{array} \qquad \begin{array}{r} 10 \\ \times\ 9 \\ \hline \end{array} \qquad \begin{array}{r} 10 \\ \times\ 3 \\ \hline \end{array}$$

2.
$$\begin{array}{r} 10 \\ \times\ 6 \\ \hline \end{array} \qquad \begin{array}{r} 10 \\ \times 10 \\ \hline \end{array} \qquad \begin{array}{r} 10 \\ \times\ 2 \\ \hline \end{array} \qquad \begin{array}{r} 10 \\ \times\ 5 \\ \hline \end{array} \qquad \begin{array}{r} 10 \\ \times\ 3 \\ \hline \end{array}$$

Multiply 5 × 3.
Then, add a zero.

$$\begin{array}{r} 50 \\ \times\ 3 \\ \hline \end{array} \qquad \begin{array}{r} 5\diagdown 0 \\ \times\ \diagdown 3 \\ \hline 150 \end{array}$$

3.
$$\begin{array}{r} 20 \\ \times\ 2 \\ \hline \end{array} \qquad \begin{array}{r} 60 \\ \times\ 7 \\ \hline \end{array} \qquad \begin{array}{r} 20 \\ \times\ 3 \\ \hline \end{array} \qquad \begin{array}{r} 40 \\ \times\ 6 \\ \hline \end{array} \qquad \begin{array}{r} 90 \\ \times\ 9 \\ \hline \end{array}$$

4.
$$\begin{array}{r} 80 \\ \times\ 5 \\ \hline \end{array} \qquad \begin{array}{r} 30 \\ \times\ 4 \\ \hline \end{array} \qquad \begin{array}{r} 70 \\ \times\ 8 \\ \hline \end{array} \qquad \begin{array}{r} 60 \\ \times\ 5 \\ \hline \end{array} \qquad \begin{array}{r} 50 \\ \times\ 4 \\ \hline \end{array}$$

☐ I can use strategies to multiply one-digit numbers by multiples of 10.

Name_____

Complete the chart. Then, answer the question.

×	10	20	30	40	50	60	70	80	90
1									
2									
3									
4									
5									
6									
7									
8									
9									

Describe a pattern you see in the chart._____

_____

☐ I can use strategies to multiply one-digit numbers by multiples of 10.
☐ I can identify and explain patterns.

Name_____

Cross out any shapes that are not divided into equal parts. Then, write the correct fraction for each remaining shape.

1. 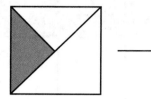 ____

2. 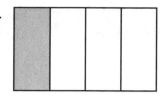 ____

3. 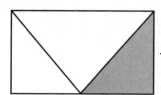 ____

4. 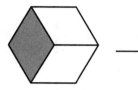 ____

5.  ____

6. 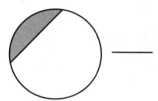 ____

Answer each question.

7. Claire says that the following shape shows $\frac{1}{3}$. Wyatt says that it does not. Who is correct? Explain.

_____

_____

8. Kade was asked to draw $\frac{3}{4}$ in two different ways. Did he draw the fractions correctly? Explain.

 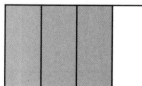

_____

_____

☐ I can recognize fractions as parts of a whole.
☐ I understand the difference between numerators and denominators.

A fraction tells about equal parts of a whole.
The top number tells how many parts are shaded.
The bottom number tells how many parts in all.

Parts shaded ⟶ $\dfrac{1}{6}$
Parts in all ⟶

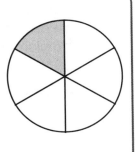

Write each fraction.

1.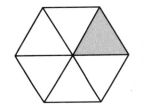

2.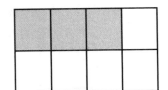

3.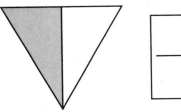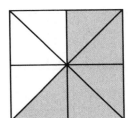

4.

5.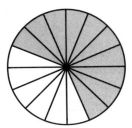

6.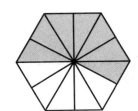

☐ I can recognize fractions as parts of a whole.
☐ I understand the difference between numerators and denominators.

A fraction tells about equal parts of a whole.
The numerator tells how many parts are shaded.
The denominator tells how many parts in all.

Parts shaded ⟶ $\dfrac{2}{6}$ ⟵ Parts in all

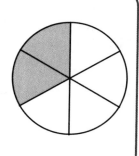

Write each fraction.

1.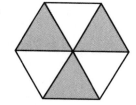

2.

3.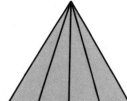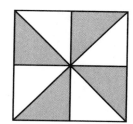

4.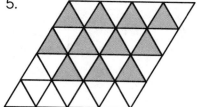

5.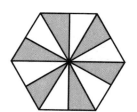

6.

☐ I can recognize fractions as parts of a whole.
☐ I understand the difference between numerators and denominators.

To find fractions of a whole and a set, ask yourself these questions:

Fractions of a Whole

 $\dfrac{4}{8}$ numerator / denominator

How many parts are shaded?
4 (numerator)

How many parts is this whole figure divided into? 8 (denominator)

Fractions of a Set

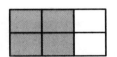 $\dfrac{6}{12}$ numerator / denominator

How many figures are shaded?
6 (numerator)

How many figures are in the set in all?
12 (denominator)

What fraction of each figure is shaded?

1.

_____

2.

_____

3.
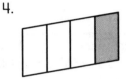
_____

4.

_____

5.

_____

6.

_____

7.

_____

8.

_____

9.
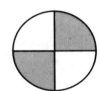
_____

10.
_____

What fraction of each set is shaded?

11.

_____

12.

_____

13.

_____

14.

_____

15.

_____

☐ I can recognize fractions as parts of a whole.
☐ I understand the difference between numerators and denominators.

Name_____

Solve each problem.

1. Holly built a new door for her tree house. What fraction of her door is not a window?

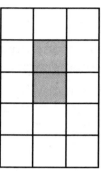

_____

2. The third-grade class built a garden outside. What fraction of the garden is tomatoes?

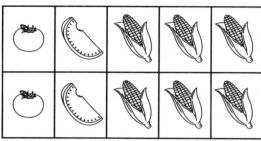

_____

3. In a paper bag were 2 blue marbles, 3 red marbles, and 2 yellow marbles. What fraction of the marbles were red or yellow?

_____

4. A teacher graded 8 tests. Half of the test grades were As, 3 were Bs, and 1 was a C. What fraction of the tests were As or Bs?

_____

5. The school has a new sidewalk around the playground. What fraction of the playground area is the sidewalk?

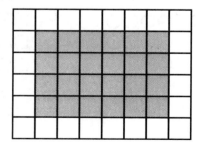

_____

6. What fraction of the word *fraction* is vowels?

Fraction

_____

☐ I can recognize fractions as parts of a whole.
☐ I understand the difference between numerators and denominators.

Cut out the fraction strips. Use them to help you label the number line.

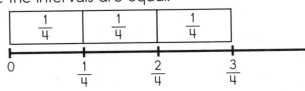

Make sure the fraction strips start at 0.
Make sure the intervals are equal.

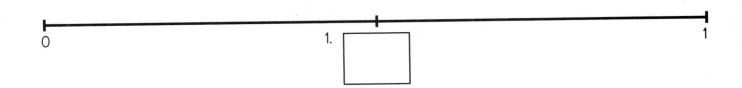

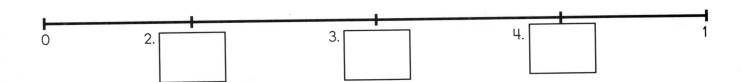

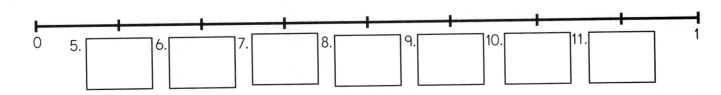

☐ I understand that fractions can be represented on a number line.
☐ I can represent a fraction on a number line from 0 to 1.

cut ✂

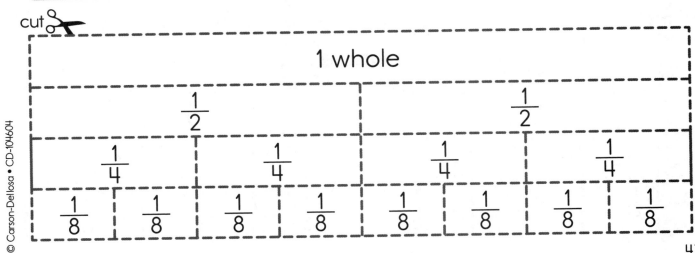

3.NF.2a

Cut out the fraction strips. Use them to help you label the number line.

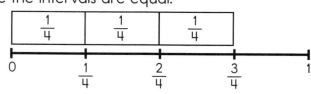

Make sure the fraction strips start at 0.
Make sure the intervals are equal.

| $\frac{1}{4}$ | $\frac{1}{4}$ | $\frac{1}{4}$ |

0    $\frac{1}{4}$ $\frac{2}{4}$ $\frac{3}{4}$ 1

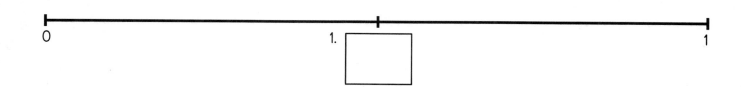

0 ————————————— 1.[ ] ————————————— 1

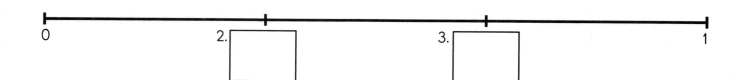

0 ———— 2.[ ] ———— 3.[ ] ———— 1

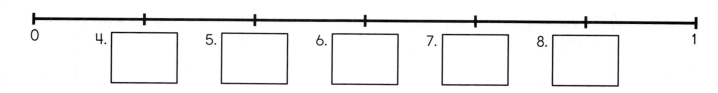

0   4.[ ]   5.[ ]   6.[ ]   7.[ ]   8.[ ]   1

☐ I understand that fractions can be represented on a number line.
☐ I can represent a fraction on a number line from 0 to 1.

cut ✂

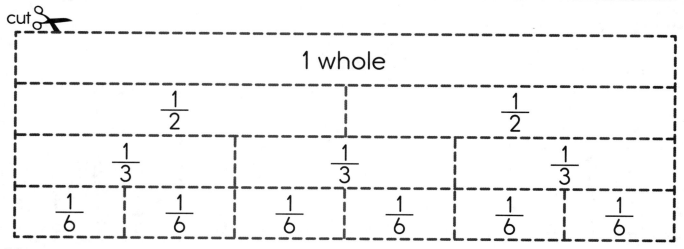

1 whole

| $\frac{1}{2}$ | $\frac{1}{2}$ |

| $\frac{1}{3}$ | $\frac{1}{3}$ | $\frac{1}{3}$ |

| $\frac{1}{6}$ | $\frac{1}{6}$ | $\frac{1}{6}$ | $\frac{1}{6}$ | $\frac{1}{6}$ | $\frac{1}{6}$ |

Mark and label each fraction on the number line. Use the fraction strips to help you.

Make sure the fraction strips start at 0.
Make sure the intervals are equal.

$\frac{1}{4}$	$\frac{1}{4}$	$\frac{1}{4}$

0      $\frac{1}{4}$ $\frac{2}{4}$ $\frac{3}{4}$ 1

1. 0, $\frac{1}{2}$, 1

2. 0, $\frac{1}{4}$, $\frac{2}{4}$, $\frac{3}{4}$, 1

3. 0, $\frac{1}{8}$, $\frac{2}{8}$, $\frac{3}{8}$, $\frac{4}{8}$, $\frac{5}{8}$, $\frac{6}{8}$, $\frac{7}{8}$, 1

☐ I understand that fractions can be represented on a number line.
☐ I can divide a number line into equal parts to represent a fraction on a number line.

cut ✂

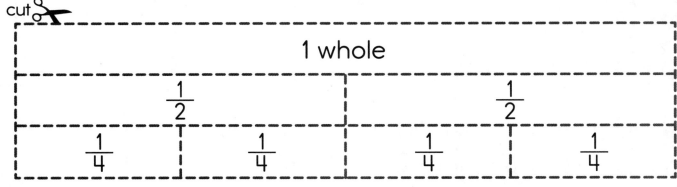

3.NF.2b

Mark and label each fraction on the number line. Use the fraction strips to help you.

Make sure the fraction strips start at 0.
Make sure the intervals are equal.

| $\frac{1}{3}$ | $\frac{1}{3}$ |

0          $\frac{1}{3}$ $\frac{2}{3}$ 1

1. 0, $\frac{1}{2}$, 1

2. 0, $\frac{1}{3}$, $\frac{2}{3}$, 1

3. 0, $\frac{1}{6}$, $\frac{2}{6}$, $\frac{3}{6}$, $\frac{4}{6}$, $\frac{5}{6}$, 1

☐ I understand that fractions can be represented on a number line.
☐ I can divide a number line into equal parts to represent a fraction on a number line.

cut ✂

1 whole					
$\frac{1}{2}$			$\frac{1}{2}$		
$\frac{1}{3}$		$\frac{1}{3}$		$\frac{1}{3}$	
$\frac{1}{6}$	$\frac{1}{6}$	$\frac{1}{6}$	$\frac{1}{6}$	$\frac{1}{6}$	$\frac{1}{6}$

Name_____

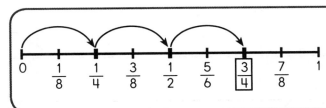

The denominator is the number of intervals in all.

The numerator is the number of intervals passed.

Label each number line.

1.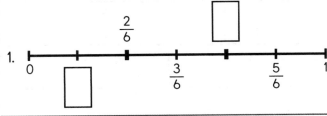

2.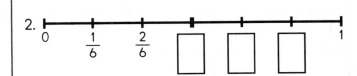

3.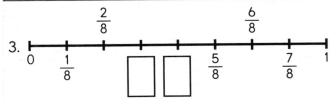

4.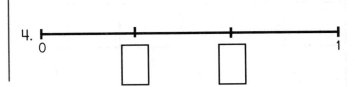

Label each number line with the fractions.

5. fourths and eighths

6. thirds and sixths

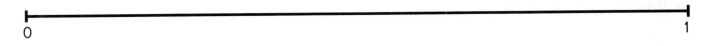

7. Explain how you know your number lines are correct.

_____

_____

_____

☐ I understand that fractions can be represented on a number line.
☐ I can represent a fraction on a number line from 0 to 1.
☐ I can divide a number line into equal parts to represent a fraction on a number line.

Name_____

Use the chart to answer each question.

$\frac{1}{1}$							
$\frac{1}{2}$				$\frac{2}{2}$			
$\frac{1}{3}$		$\frac{2}{3}$			$\frac{3}{3}$		
$\frac{1}{4}$		$\frac{2}{4}$		$\frac{3}{4}$		$\frac{4}{4}$	
$\frac{1}{5}$	$\frac{2}{5}$		$\frac{3}{5}$		$\frac{4}{5}$		$\frac{5}{5}$
$\frac{1}{6}$	$\frac{2}{6}$	$\frac{3}{6}$		$\frac{4}{6}$	$\frac{5}{6}$		$\frac{6}{6}$
$\frac{1}{7}$	$\frac{2}{7}$	$\frac{3}{7}$	$\frac{4}{7}$	$\frac{5}{7}$	$\frac{6}{7}$		$\frac{7}{7}$
$\frac{1}{8}$	$\frac{2}{8}$	$\frac{3}{8}$	$\frac{4}{8}$	$\frac{5}{8}$	$\frac{6}{8}$	$\frac{7}{8}$	$\frac{8}{8}$

1. Look at the fifth row. How many fifths equal 1 whole? _____

2. Which fractions shown are equal to $\frac{1}{2}$? _____

3. Which fraction shown is equal to $\frac{1}{3}$?_____

4. Which is greater: $\frac{2}{7}$ or $\frac{3}{6}$?_____

5. Which is less: $\frac{7}{8}$ or $\frac{3}{4}$? _____

6. Which fraction shown is equal to $\frac{3}{4}$?_____

7. Which fraction is greater: $\frac{1}{4}$ or $\frac{2}{6}$?_____

8. Write all of the fractions shown that are equal to 1._____

☐ I can compare fractions.
☐ I understand what makes fractions equivalent.

Fractions that equal the same amount are called **equivalent fractions.**
Example:

$$\frac{1}{2} = \frac{2}{4}$$

Write the equivalent fractions.

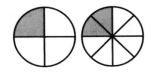

1. _____ = _____

2. _____ = _____

3. _____ = _____

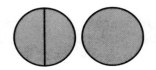

4. _____ = _____

5. _____ = _____

6. _____ = _____

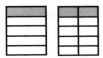

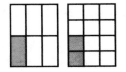

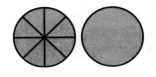

7. _____ = _____

8. _____ = _____

9. _____ = _____

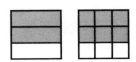

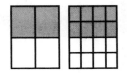

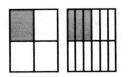

10. _____ = _____

11. _____ = _____

12. _____ = _____

☐ I can compare fractions.
☐ I understand what makes fractions equivalent.

Write the correct fractions.

1. 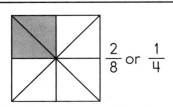 $\frac{2}{8}$ or $\frac{1}{4}$

2. _____ or _____

3. _____ or _____

4. _____ or _____

5. _____ or _____

Shade in the shapes to make equivalent fractions.

6. $\frac{1}{2}$ or $\frac{2}{4}$ = $\frac{4}{8}$

7. $\frac{2}{3}$ or $\frac{4}{6}$ = _____

8. $\frac{1}{3}$ = _____

Write the fraction for the shaded part above each shape. Then, write the fraction for the unshaded part below each shape. Circle the greater fraction.

9. $\frac{1}{6}$ 10. ___   11. ___   12. ___   13. ___   14. ___

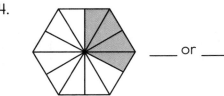

$\boxed{\frac{5}{6}}$ ___   ___   ___   ___   ___

$\frac{1}{2} = \frac{\boxed{2}}{4}$ $\frac{1}{2} = \frac{3}{\boxed{6}}$

Equivalent fractions are fractions that are equal. Draw pictures to find equivalent fractions.

Draw a picture of each fraction. Write the missing numbers to show equivalent fractions.

1. $\frac{1}{3} = \frac{\square}{6}$

2. $\frac{1}{4} = \frac{\square}{8}$

3. $\frac{2}{3} = \frac{\square}{6}$

4. $\frac{3}{4} = \frac{6}{\square}$

5. $\frac{6}{8} = \frac{3}{\square}$

6. $\frac{4}{6} = \frac{\square}{3}$

7. $\frac{2}{4} = \frac{1}{\square}$

8. $\frac{1}{2} = \frac{\square}{4} = \frac{3}{\square} = \frac{\square}{8}$

☐ I can compare fractions.
☐ I can recognize and form simple equivalent fractions.

Name_____

Solve each problem.

1. Explain how the number line shows equivalent fractions.

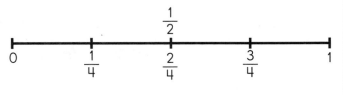

_____

_____

2. Complete the number line to show that $\frac{1}{3}$ and $\frac{2}{6}$ are equivalent.

```
|——————————————————————————|
0                          1
```

3. Which fractions are equivalent?

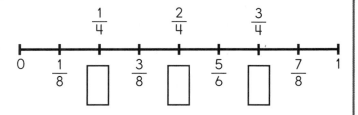

4. Which fractions are equivalent to 1 whole?

_____

Explain how you know they are equivalent.

_____

_____

_____

5. Juan says that $\frac{5}{8}$ and $\frac{1}{2}$ are equivalent.

   Is he correct? Explain why or why not. Draw a number line to help you.

_____

_____

6. Tell what an equivalent fraction is in your own words.

_____

_____

_____

_____

☐ **I can compare fractions.**
☐ **I can recognize and form simple equivalent fractions.**

Name_____

Write the missing numbers to show equivalent fractions.

 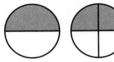

$\frac{1}{2} \times \frac{(2)}{(2)} = \frac{2}{4}$ $\frac{1}{2} \times \frac{(3)}{(3)} = \frac{3}{6}$

Equivalent fractions are fractions that are equal. To find equivalent fractions, multiply the numerator and the denominator of a fraction by the same number.

1. $\frac{1}{3} \times \frac{(\ \ )}{(2)} = \frac{}{6}$

2. $\frac{4}{5} \times \frac{(2)}{(\ \ )} = \frac{8}{}$

3. $\frac{1}{4} \times \frac{(\ \ )}{(2)} = \frac{}{8}$

4. $\frac{2}{5} \times \frac{(\ \ )}{(4)} = \frac{}{20}$

5. $\frac{2}{3} \times \frac{(\ \ )}{(3)} = \frac{}{9}$

6. $\frac{3}{4} \times \frac{(\ \ )}{(3)} = \frac{}{12}$

7. $\frac{3}{4} \times \frac{(\ \ )}{(4)} = \frac{}{16}$

8. $\frac{5}{6} \times \frac{(\ \ )}{(3)} = \frac{}{18}$

9. $\frac{4}{7} \times \frac{(4)}{(\ \ )} = \frac{16}{}$

10. $\frac{3}{4} \times \frac{(7)}{(\ \ )} = \frac{21}{}$

11. $\frac{7}{8} \times \frac{(5)}{(\ \ )} = \frac{35}{}$

12. $\frac{5}{6} \times \frac{(\ \ )}{(4)} = \frac{}{24}$

☐ I can compare fractions.
☐ I can recognize and form simple equivalent fractions.

Write each whole number as a fraction.

Example:

$3 = \dfrac{12}{4}$

1.
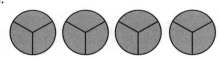

$4 =$ ——

2.

$2 =$ ——

3.

$2 =$ ——

4.
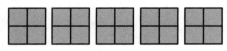

$5 =$ ——

5.
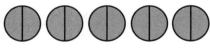

$5 =$ ——

6.

$4 =$ ——

7.
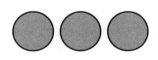

$3 =$ ——

8.

$4 =$ ——

9.

$2 =$ ——

Draw a picture to show each number as a fraction. Then, write each whole number as a fraction.

10. 6

11. 3

12. 8

13. 10

14. 7

15. 9

☐ I can compare fractions.
☐ I can express whole numbers as fractions.

Name_____

Write each fraction as a whole number. Draw a picture to help you.

1. $\frac{12}{3}$ = ___4___   2. $\frac{10}{2}$ = _____

3. $\frac{16}{4}$ = _____   4. $\frac{12}{2}$ = _____

5. $\frac{16}{8}$ = _____   6. $\frac{20}{4}$ = _____

7. $\frac{28}{4}$ = _____   8. $\frac{21}{3}$ = _____

9. $\frac{16}{2}$ = _____   10. $\frac{36}{4}$ = _____

11. $\frac{9}{3}$ = _____   12. $\frac{40}{8}$ = _____

13. $\frac{22}{2}$ = _____   14. $\frac{30}{3}$ = _____

15. $\frac{40}{4}$ = _____   16. $\frac{36}{6}$ = _____

☐ I can compare fractions.
☐ I can express whole numbers as fractions.

Name_____

Look at each number line. Write the fraction that is equivalent to 1 whole.

1. 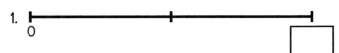 □

2. 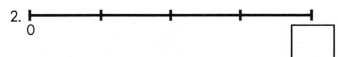 □

3. 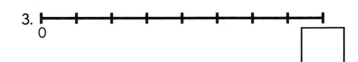 □

4. 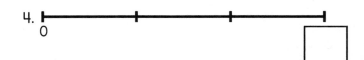 □

5. ├──┼──┼──┼──┼──┼──┼──┤
   0   □

6. Explain how you know the fractions are equivalent to 1 whole.

   _____

   _____

Draw a number line. Label it with the fractions.

7. $0, \frac{1}{2}, \frac{1}{4}, \frac{2}{4}, \frac{3}{4}, \frac{4}{4}, \frac{1}{8}, \frac{2}{8}, \frac{3}{8}, \frac{4}{8}, \frac{5}{8}, \frac{6}{8}, \frac{7}{8}, \frac{8}{8}, 1$

8. $0, \frac{1}{2}, \frac{1}{3}, \frac{2}{3}, \frac{3}{3}, \frac{4}{4}, \frac{1}{6}, \frac{2}{6}, \frac{3}{6}, \frac{4}{6}, \frac{5}{6}, \frac{6}{6}, 1$

☐ I understand what makes fractions equivalent.
☐ I can express whole number as fractions.
☐ I understand that fractions can be represented on a number line.
☐ I can divide a number line into equal parts to represent a fraction on a number line.

Name_____

To compare fractions, determine which figure has more area shaded. If necessary, find equivalent fractions and compare the numerators.

$\frac{1}{2} = \frac{3}{6}$

$\frac{1}{3} = \frac{2}{6}$

$\frac{1}{2}$ $\frac{1}{3}$ $\frac{3}{6}$ $\frac{2}{6}$

Write the correct fractions. Then, write <, >, or = to compare each pair of fractions.

1.

_____ ◯ _____

2.

_____ ◯ _____

3.

_____ ◯ _____

4.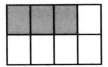

_____ ◯ _____

5.

_____ ◯ _____

6.

_____ ◯ _____

☐ I can compare fractions.
☐ I can compare fractions that have the same numerator or the same denominator.
☐ I can justify the comparisons.

Name_____

Draw a picture of each fraction. Write >, <, or = to compare each pair of fractions.

1. $\frac{1}{3}$ ◯ $\frac{3}{3}$

2. $\frac{1}{4}$ ◯ $\frac{3}{4}$

3. $\frac{4}{6}$ ◯ $\frac{1}{6}$

4. $\frac{1}{2}$ ◯ $\frac{2}{2}$

5. $\frac{7}{8}$ ◯ $\frac{5}{8}$

6. $\frac{2}{4}$ ◯ $\frac{1}{4}$

7. Each pair of fractions above has the same denominator.

Complete this statement: If the denominators are the same, the fraction with the smaller numerator is _____ .

8. $\frac{2}{2}$ ◯ $\frac{2}{3}$

9. $\frac{1}{6}$ ◯ $\frac{1}{3}$

10. $\frac{4}{8}$ ◯ $\frac{4}{4}$

11. $\frac{1}{3}$ ◯ $\frac{1}{2}$

12. $\frac{3}{6}$ ◯ $\frac{3}{8}$

13. $\frac{5}{6}$ ◯ $\frac{5}{8}$

14. Each pair of fractions above has the same numerator.

Complete this statement: If the numerators are the same, the fraction with the smaller denominator is _____ .

☐ I can compare fractions.
☐ I can compare fractions that have the same numerator or the same denominator.
☐ I can justify the comparisons.

Name_____

There are five minutes between each number on a clock.

We read the time on this clock as **nine seventeen**.

We write the time as **9:17**.

Write the time shown on each clock.

1.
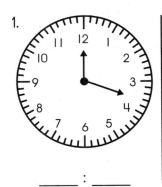
____ : ____

2.

____ : ____

3.
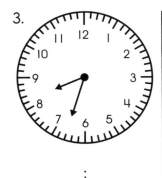
____ : ____

4.

____ : ____

Draw hands on each clock to show the time.

5.
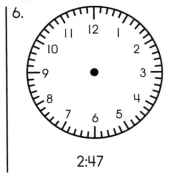
8:23

6.
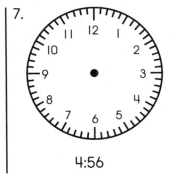
2:47

7.
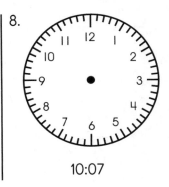
4:56

8.

10:07

□ I can tell and write time to the nearest minute.

Name_____

Write the time shown on each clock.

1.

_____ : _____

2.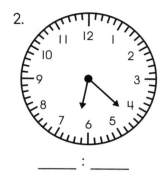

_____ : _____

3.

_____ : _____

4.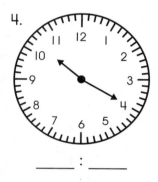

_____ : _____

5.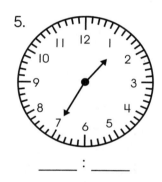

_____ : _____

6.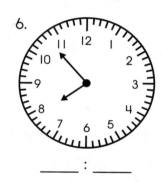

_____ : _____

7.

_____ : _____

8.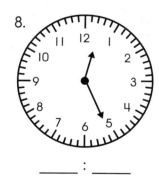

_____ : _____

9.

_____ : _____

☐ I can tell and write time to the nearest minute.

Name_____

Draw hands on each clock to show the time.

1.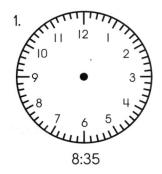

8:35

2.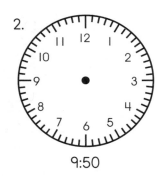

9:50

3.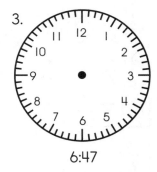

6:47

4.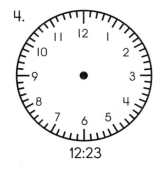

12:23

5.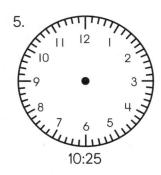

10:25

6.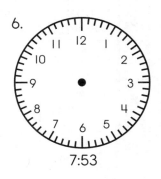

7:53

7.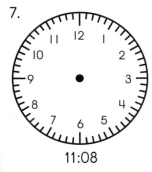

11:08

8.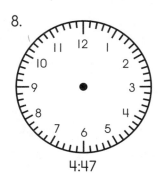

4:47

9.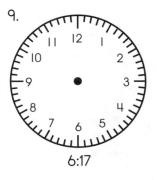

6:17

☐ I can tell and write time to the nearest minute.

Name_____

Use the chart to answer each question.

To find elapsed time, you can either draw a clock or a number line.

 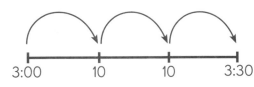

3:00   10   10   3:30

	7:00	7:30	8:00	8:30	9:00	9:30	10:00	10:30
2	Million Dollar Game Show	Jump Start		News Magazine			News	
4	Lucky Guess	You Should Know	Wednesday Night at the Movies "Friends Forever"				News	
5	Best Friends	Sarah's Secret	Where They Are	Time to Hope	Tom's Talk Show		News	
7	Helping Out	Lost Alone	Last One Standing	Sports Tonight			News	
11	Your Health	Eating Right	Nutrition News		Cooking with Kate		Home Decorating	Shopping Show
24	Silly Rabbit	Clyde the Clown	Your Lucky Day	Slime and Rhyme	Cartoon Alley		Fun Times	Make Me Laugh

1. What information does this chart provide? _____

2. How much time does this chart cover on Wednesday night? _____

3. How long is it from the start of *Your Health* until the end of *Nutrition News*? _____

_____

4. If John started watching the Channel 7 news 15 minutes late, how long did he watch the

news? _____

5. How long is the Wednesday night movie on Channel 4? _____

6. If Nikki watched *Best Friends* and *Cartoon Alley*, how long did she spend watching TV?

_____

☐ I can tell and write time to the nearest minute.
☐ I can solve time problems.

66

Use the time shown on each clock to answer the questions.

1.

What time does the clock show? _____

What time would it be if it were 20 minutes earlier? _____

What time will it be in 3 hours and 35 minutes? _____

What time will it be in 65 minutes? _____

2.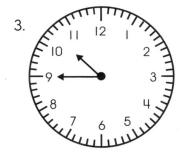

What time does the clock show? _____

What time would it be if it were 48 minutes earlier? _____

What time will it be in 5 hours and 22 minutes? _____

What time will it be in 57 minutes? _____

3.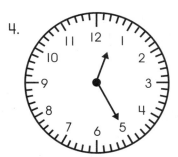

What time does the clock show? _____

What time would it be if it were 8 hours and 15 minutes earlier? _____

What time will it be in 4 hours and 15 minutes? _____

What time will it be in 75 minutes? _____

4.

What time does the clock show? _____

What time would it be if it were 9 hours earlier? _____

What time will it be in 9 hours and 6 minutes? _____

What time will it be in 3 hours and 47 minutes? _____

☐ I can tell and write time to the nearest minute.
☐ I can solve time problems.

Answer each question.

1. Isabella wants to watch a show at 8:00 pm. It is 7:23 pm. How many minutes does she have to wait before the show starts?

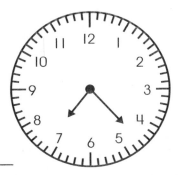

_____

2. Cade's favorite show starts at 7:30 pm. It is 90 minutes long. What time will the show end?

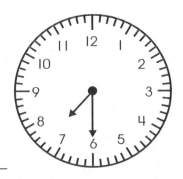

_____

3. Taylor's favorite show started at 4:30 pm. It is 30 minutes long. It is now 4:53 pm. In how many minutes does the show end?

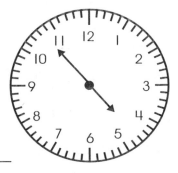

_____

4. Monique watched a movie that started at 7:00 pm. It lasted 1 hour and 47 minutes. What time did the movie end?

_____

5. Jonathan started watching a show at 4:16 pm. He turned the TV off at 5:37 pm. How long did he watch TV?

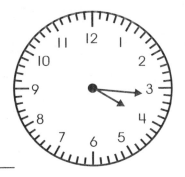

_____

6. Chelsea watched two 30-minute shows on Monday, one 30-minute show on Wednesday, and three 30-minute shows on Friday. How many hours of TV did she watch that week?

_____

☐ I can tell and write time to the nearest minute.
☐ I can solve time problems.

Answer each question.

1. Adam gets up at 7:30. It takes him 25 minutes to get ready for school. What time does he leave for school?

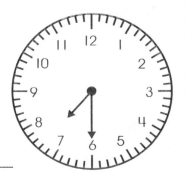

_____

2. Adam has piano lessons on Mondays. His piano lessons start at 4:15. The lessons are 25 minutes long. What time does Adam finish his lessons?

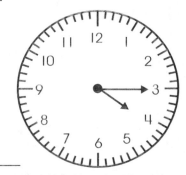

_____

3. It takes Adam 7 minutes to ride his bike to a friend's house. Today, he left home at 3:17. What time will he get to his friend's house?

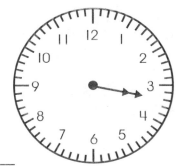

_____

4. On Wednesday, Adam arrived at his friend's house at 4:13. They played for 1 hour and 30 minutes. What time did Adam go home?

_____

5. Adam knows it takes him 9 minutes to wash his face, brush his teeth, and get ready for bed. His parents want him in bed at 8:30. What time does Adam need to start getting ready for bed?

_____

6. Adam goes to bed at 8:30 at night and sleeps until 7:30 the next morning. How many hours of sleep does he get?

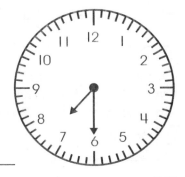

_____

☐ I can tell and write time to the nearest minute.
☐ I can solve time problems.

Answer each question. Each question is related to the one before it, so complete them in order. Use *am* and *pm* to specify the time of day.

1. India gets up every morning at 6:30 am. It takes her 20 minutes to shower and get dressed. Then, she eats breakfast in 15 minutes. After breakfast, she does chores. What time does she start her chores?

   _____7:05am_____

2. After eating breakfast and showering, it takes India 5 minutes to feed the dog. Then, she takes him for a walk for 30 minutes. What time is it now?

   _____

3. Next, India sits and reads for 45 minutes. Then, she has to leave for school. What time is it when India leaves?

   _____

4. It takes India 20 minutes to walk to school. What time does she get to school?

   _____

5. India is at school for 6 ½ hours. Then, she walks home. What time should she get home from school? Remember, it took India 20 minutes to walk to school.

   _____

6. India takes 5 minutes to change her clothes and 5 minutes to eat a snack. She rides her bike to soccer practice. It takes her about 10 minutes to get there. What time does she arrive at practice?

   _____

7. The practice lasts 1 hour and 15 minutes. What time is practice over?

   _____

8. India rides her bike home with her friend. They talk for 23 minutes about the upcoming game. Then, India puts away her bike, which takes 2 minutes. Then, she goes to the kitchen to help with dinner. What time is it now? Remember, it took her 10 minutes to ride her bike to soccer practice.

   _____

☐ I can tell and write time to the nearest minute.
☐ I can solve time problems.

Name_____

Capacity is the amount a container can hold when it is full.

1 liter (L) =

1 milliliter (mL) =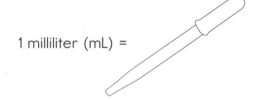

Choose the best unit to measure each item.

1. The capacity of a bathtub
   A. L   B. mL

2. The amount of juice in a juice box
   A. L   B. mL

3. The capacity of a canned soft drink
   A. L   B. mL

4. The amount of water in a large bucket
   A. L   B. mL

5. The amount of oil in a teaspoon
   A. L   B. mL

6. One swimming pool can hold 58 L of water, while another can hold 73 L. What is the difference?

   _____

7. Mom bought 12 L of apple juice for the party. Dad bought 9 L more. How many liters did they buy in all?

   _____

8. At the snack counter, 1 cup can hold 215 mL of water. How much water can 3 cups hold?

   _____

9. Suzy had 10 L of water. She wanted to pour an equal amount of water into 5 thermoses. How many liters did she pour into each thermos?

   _____

☐ I can measure volume and mass using customary and metric units.
☐ I can solve volume and mass problems.

Mass is the amount of matter in an object.

1 gram (g) =

1 kilogram (kg) =

Choose the best unit to measure each item.

1. The mass of a strawberry
   A. g   B. kg

2. The mass of a full suitcase
   A. g   B. kg

3. The amount of matter in a bowling ball
   A. g   B. kg

4. The amount of matter in a pushpin
   A. g   B. kg

5. The mass of an apple
   A. g   B. kg

6. Jawan put some apples in a bowl. Each apple had a mass of 200 g. The total mass of all of the apples was 800 g. How many apples were in the bowl?

   _____

7. The computer's mass was 5 kg, and the printer's mass was 2 kg. How much mass did they have in all?

   _____

8. The moped weighed 15 kg, while the bike weighed 3 kg. How much more mass did the moped have than the bike?

   _____

9. Which object probably has more mass: a baseball or a golf ball? Explain.

   _____

☐ I can measure volume and mass using customary and metric units.
☐ I can solve volume and mass problems.

Name_____

Bar graphs can be used to display and compare information. The bar graph below shows the results of a science experiment to find the best plant food.

Use the bar graph to answer each question.

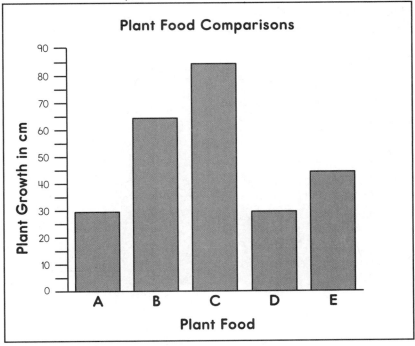

1. How much did the plant that received food B grow? _____

2. Which two plant foods produced the same growth?

_____ and _____

3. How much more did the plant that received food C grow than the plant that received food A?

_____

4. How much did the plant that received food E grow? _____

5. Which two plant foods produced 110 cm of growth altogether?

_____ and _____

6. How much more did the plant that received food B grow than the plant that received food D?

_____

☐ I can read a scaled bar graph with multiple categories.
☐ I can analyze graphs to solve problems.

> **Pictographs** use pictures to display and compare information. The pictograph below shows the results of a food drive at Lindy Elementary School.

Use the pictograph to answer each question.

Lindy Elementary Food Drive

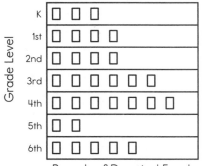

Each ☐ stands for 60 pounds of donated food.

Pounds of Donated Food

1. Which grade level donated the most pounds of food? _____

2. Which grade level donated 120 pounds of food? _____

3. What was the total amount of food donated by the entire school?

   _____

4. How many more pounds of food did grade 4 donate than grade 5?

   _____

5. Who donated more food, grade 1 or grade 6? _____

6. How many more pounds of food did grade K donate than grade 5?

   _____

7. Which grade level donated a total of 300 pounds of food? _____

8. How many pounds of food did grades 3 and 4 donate altogether?

   _____

> ☐ I can read a scaled picture graph with multiple categories.
> ☐ I can analyze graphs to solve problems.

74

Name_____

Pictographs use pictures to compare information. **Bar graphs** use bars to compare information.

The pictograph below shows the types of frozen treats eaten at Armstrong Elementary. The Food Bank Volunteers bar graph shows the number of volunteers at two different schools.

Use the graphs to answer each question.

Favorite Frozen Fruit Treats at Armstrong Elementary

Type of Frozen Treat	
Grape	▭ ▭ ▯
Orange	▭ ▭ ▯
Cranberry	▭ ▭ ▭
Cherry	▭ ▭ ▭ ▭
Strawberry	▭ ▭ ▭ ▭ ▭
Kiwi	▭ ▭ ▭
Apple	▭

Number of Frozen Treats Eaten

▭ = 12 frozen fruit treats

▯ = 6 frozen fruit treats

Food Bank Volunteers

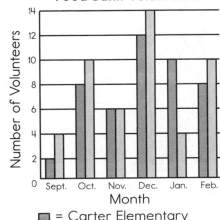

□ = Carter Elementary

□ = Madison Elementary

1. Which flavor was the most popular?

_____

2. Which two flavors were half as popular as the most popular flavor?

_____

3. Which flavor was the least popular?

_____

4. Which flavor was the second most popular?

_____

5. Which school had more volunteers in December?

_____

6. What was the total number of volunteers at that school for December?

_____

7. How many more volunteers helped from Carter Elementary than from Madison Elementary in January?

_____

8. Which school had more volunteers in October?

_____

☐ I can read a scaled picture graph and a scaled bar graph with multiple categories.
☐ I can analyze graphs to solve problems.

Name_____

Measure to the nearest quarter inch.

1.

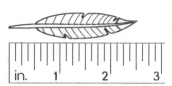

2.

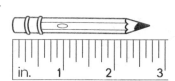

3.

4.

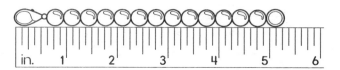

5.

6.

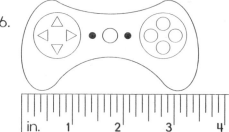

7.

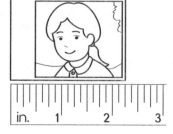

8.

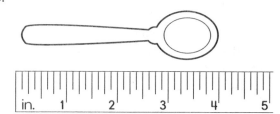

9.

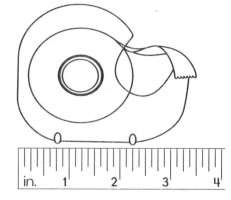

10.

To-do List
- clean

☐ I can gather data on lengths measured in inches, half inches, and quarter inches.
☐ I can show the data on a line plot.

76

Name_____

Use a ruler to measure to the nearest quarter inch.

1.	2.	3. 
4. 	5. 	6.
7.	8.	9.

10. Use the measurements to complete the line plot.

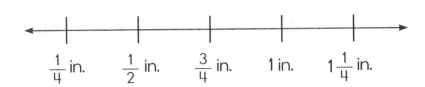

$\frac{1}{4}$ in. $\frac{1}{2}$ in. $\frac{3}{4}$ in.   1 in. $1\frac{1}{4}$ in.

11. Which measurements occurred most frequently? _____

12. Which measurement occurred least frequently? _____

13. How many more objects measured 1 in. than $\frac{1}{4}$ in.? _____

14. How many objects did you measure in all? _____

- ☐ I can gather data on lengths measured in inches, half inches, and quarter inches.
- ☐ I can show the data on a line plot.
- ☐ I can analyze a line plot to solve problems.

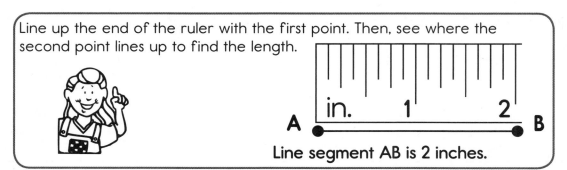

Line up the end of the ruler with the first point. Then, see where the second point lines up to find the length.

in.   1   2

A   B

Line segment AB is 2 inches.

Use a ruler to measure to the nearest quarter inch.

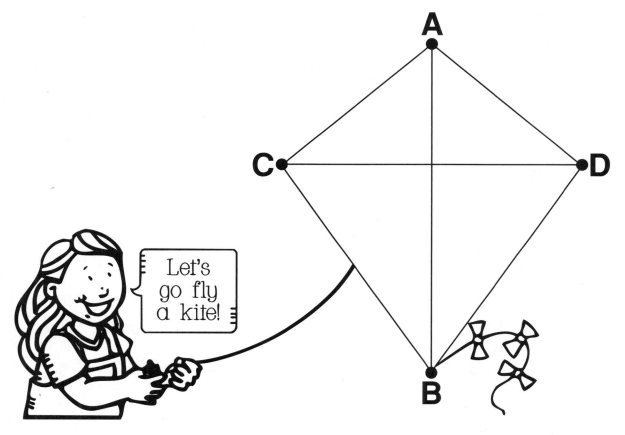

Let's go fly a kite!

1.   Line segment AB _____ in.

2.   Line segment AD _____ in.

3.   Line segment CD _____ in.

4.   Line segment BD _____ in.

5.   Line segment AC _____ in.

6.   Line segment BC _____ in.

☐ I can gather data on lengths measured in inches, half inches, and quarter inches.
☐ I can show the data on a line plot.

Name_____

Area is the number of square units inside a figure. To find the area, count the number of squares it takes to cover the figure.

Six squares are inside the figure, so the area is 6 square units

Area = 6 square units

Count the squares to find the area of each figure.

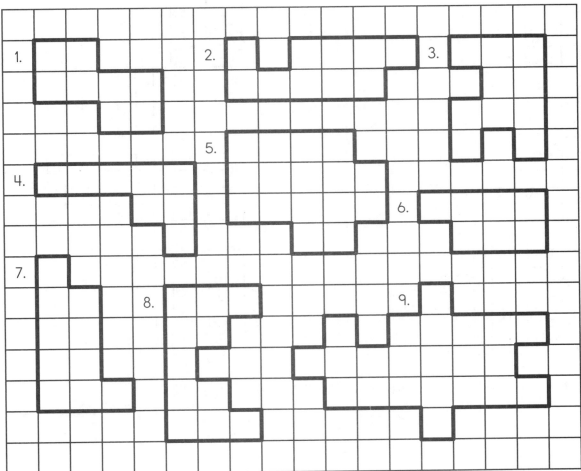

1. Area = _____ cm²

2. Area = _____ cm²

3. Area = _____ cm²

4. Area = _____ cm²

5. Area = _____ cm²

6. Area = _____ cm²

7. Area = _____ cm²

8. Area = _____ cm²

9. Area = _____ cm²

☐ I understand area.
☐ I can find area by using square units laid side by side without gaps or overlaps.
☐ I can find area by counting square units.

Name_____

When drawing square units to find the area, □ = 1 square unit
- there should be no gaps;
- there should be no overlapping.

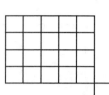 = 9 square units

Find the area.

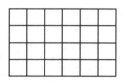

1. _____

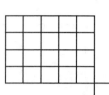

2. _____

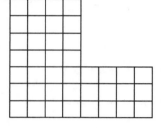

3. _____

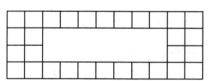

4. _____

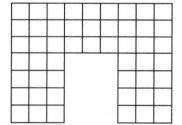

5. _____

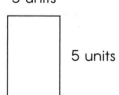

6. _____

Draw each number of square units. Then, find the area.

4 units
4 units

6 units
2 units

3 units
5 units

7. _____

8. _____

9. _____

□ I understand area.
□ I can find area by using square units laid side by side without gaps or overlaps.
□ I can find area by counting square units.

Name_____

Area is the number of square units enclosed within a boundary. To find the area of a square or a rectangle, draw square units or multiply the length by the width.

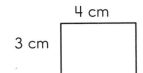

4 cm

3 cm

Area = Length x Width
A = 4 cm x 3 cm
A = 12 cm²

or

4 cm

3 cm

Find the area of each item.

12 in.

6 in.

1. A = _____ in.²

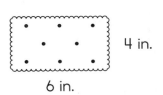

4 in.

6 in.

2. A = _____ in.²

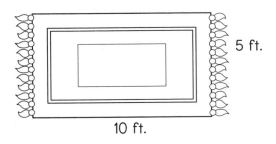

5 ft.

10 ft.

3. A = _____ ft.²

6 ft.

3 ft.

4. A = _____ ft.²

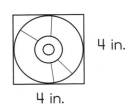

4 in.

4 in.

5. A = _____ in.²

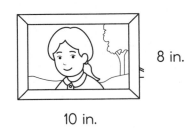

8 in.

10 in.

6. A = _____ in.²

7. Explain in your own words how to find the area of a square or a rectangle.

_____

☐ I can use multiplication and addition to solve for area.
☐ I can find the area by multiplying the side lengths.

When given a large area to calculate, you can break it into smaller sections and then use the formula (a × b) + (a × c).

4 × 15

(4 × 10) + (4 × 5)

40 + 20 = 60 sq. units

Find the area.

1.
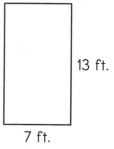

13 ft.

7 ft.

2.

5 m

20 m

3.

8 ft.

17 ft.

4.

3 in.

24 in.

You can also break apart unusual shapes to find the total area.

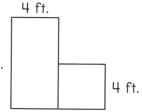

4 ft.

8 ft.

4 ft.

(8 × 4) + (4 × 4)

32 + 16 = 48 sq. ft.

5.
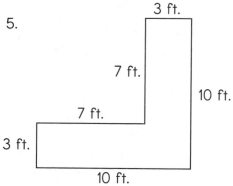

3 ft.

7 ft.

7 ft.

10 ft.

3 ft.

10 ft.

6.
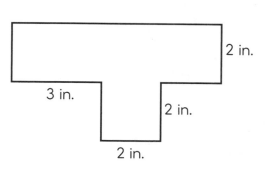

2 in.

3 in.

2 in.

2 in.

☐ I can use multiplication and addition to solve for area.
☐ I can find the area of a rectangle by using the distributive property of multiplication.
☐ I can find the area of a rectangular polygon by separating it into smaller rectangles and adding the areas.

Perimeter is the total distance around a figure. To find the perimeter, add the lengths of all of the sides.

8 cm

2 cm

P = 8 cm + 2 cm + 8 cm + 2 cm

P = 20 cm

Label the missing sides. Then, find the perimeter of each figure.

1.
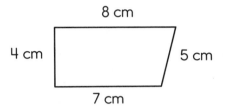
8 cm

4 cm

5 cm

7 cm

P = _____ cm

2.
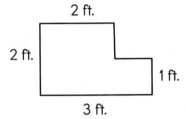
2 ft.

2 ft.

1 ft.

3 ft.

P = _____ ft.

3.
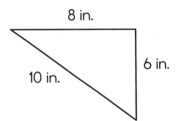
8 in.

6 in.

10 in.

P = _____ in.

4.
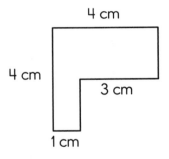
4 cm

4 cm

3 cm

1 cm

P = _____ cm

5.
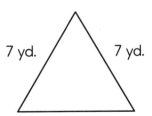
7 yd.

7 yd.

P = _____ yd.

6.
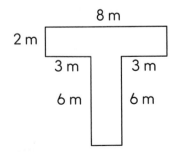
8 m

2 m

3 m

3 m

6 m

6 m

P = _____ m

☐ **I can solve for the perimeters of polygons when given various pieces of information.**

Use the diagram to answer each question.

1. What is the area of Kenny's desk? _____

    What is the perimeter?_____

2. What is the area of the fish tank? _____

    What is the perimeter?_____

3. What is the area of the closet? _____

    What is the perimeter?_____

4. What is the area of the computer center? _____

    What is the perimeter?_____

5. How many square feet do the closet and the bookcase total? _____

6. How much larger is the perimeter of Kenny's desk than Amy's desk? _____

Mrs. April's Classroom

(all measurements shown in feet)

I can solve for the perimeters of polygons.
I can use multiplication and addition to solve for area.
I can find the area by multiplying the side lengths.
I can solve problems involving areas of rectangles.

When three or more line segments come together, they form a **polygon**.

A polygon with 3 sides is a **triangle**.

A polygon with 4 sides is a **quadrilateral**.

A polygon with 5 sides is a **pentagon**.

Identify each figure as a triangle, quadrilateral, or pentagon.

1.

_____

2.

_____

3.

_____

4.

_____

5.

_____

6.

_____

7.

_____

8.

_____

9.

_____

10.

_____

11.

_____

12.

_____

☐ I understand that all shapes within a category share similar attributes.
☐ I can identify and describe shapes based on their attributes.

A **polygon** is a closed plane figure formed by three or more line segments.

Draw a line to match each polygon to its name. Explain how you know.

1.    hexagon   _____
_____
_____

2.    triangle   _____
_____
_____

3.    square   _____
_____
_____

4.   rectangle   _____
_____
_____

5. 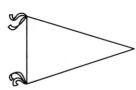   pentagon   _____
_____
_____

6. 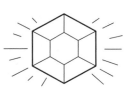   octagon   _____
_____
_____

☐ **I understand that all shapes within a category share similar attributes.**
☐ **I can identify and describe shapes based on their attributes.**

> **Parallel** lines run side by side and never cross.
> A **quadrilateral** is any shape with four sides.

Use the shapes to answer the questions.

square   rectangle   trapezoid   rhombus   circle

triangle   pentagon   hexagon   octagon

1. Name the shapes that are quadrilaterals.

   _____   _____

   _____   _____

2. What is the only quadrilateral with four equal sides?_____

3. What shape has three sides and three angles? _____

4. What shape has no sides?_____

5. What shape has five sides?_____

6. What shape has six sides? _____

7. What shape has eight sides?_____

8. What shapes have one set or more of parallel sides?

   _____   _____

   _____   _____

   _____   _____

9. How is a trapezoid different from a rhombus? _____

   _____

> ☐ I understand that all shapes within a category share similar attributes.
> ☐ I can identify and describe shapes based on their attributes.

Name_____

A **polygon** is a closed plane figure formed by three or more line segments with two sides meeting at each vertex.

parallelogram   **quadrilateral**   **square**   **rectangle**   **rhombus**   **trapezoid**

Identify each figure.

1.

_____

2.

_____

3.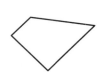

_____

4.

_____

5.

_____

6.

_____

7.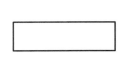

_____

8.

_____

9.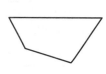

_____

10.

_____

11. What do shapes 1 to 10 have in common?

_____

_____

Draw each shape.

12. rhombus   13. rectangle   14. square

15. Draw a quadrilateral that is not a rhombus, rectangle, or square.

☐ I understand that all shapes within a category share similar attributes.
☐ I can identify and describe shapes based on their attributes.

Cross out the shapes that are not divided equally. Label how each remaining shape is divided.

1. A.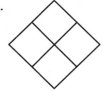

2. B.

3. C.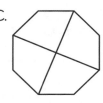

4. D.

_____   _____   _____   _____

1. A.

B.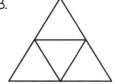

C.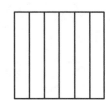

D.

_____   _____   _____   _____

Divide each shape.

2. A.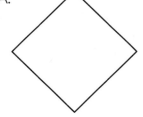

eighths

B.

halves

C.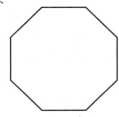

eighths

D.

tenths

3. A.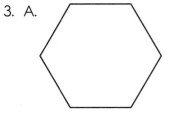

sixths

B.

thirds

C.

fourths

D.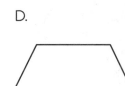

thirds

□ I can divide shapes into equal parts, using fractions to describe each part.

Name_____

 To **partition** a shape means to divide it. When showing fractions, partition shapes into equal parts.

Connect the dots to form different geometric shapes. Then, divide them into equal fractions of an area.

1.

Connect the dots to form a triangle. Divide it into fourths.

2.

Connect the dots to form a square. Divide it into fifths.

3.

Connect the dots to form a trapezoid. Divide it into halves.

4.

Connect the dots to form a rhombus. Divide it into thirds.

☐ **I can divide shapes into equal parts using unit fractions to describe each part.**

Answer Key

Page 12

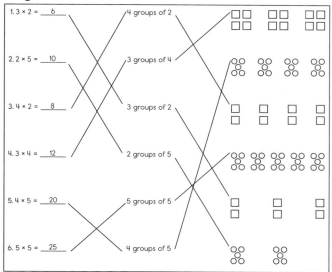

7. 16, Drawings will vary. 8. 9, Drawings will vary.

Page 13
1. 21, Answers will vary. 2. 30, Answers will vary.
3. 36, Answers will vary. 4. 72, Answers will vary.

Page 14
1. 7, Drawings will vary. 21 – 3 = 18, 18 – 3 = 15,
15 – 3 = 12, 12 – 3 = 9, 9 – 3 = 6, 6 – 3 = 3, 3 – 3
= 0; 2. 6, Drawings will vary. 30 – 5 = 25, 25 – 5
= 20, 20 – 5 = 15, 15 – 5 = 10, 10 – 5 = 5, 5 – 5 =
0; 3. 4, Drawings will vary. 36 – 9 = 27, 27 – 9 =
18, 18 – 9 = 9, 9 – 9 = 0; 4. 3, Drawings will vary.
18 – 6 = 12, 12 – 6 = 6, 6 – 6 = 0

Page 15
1. 3, Answers will vary. 2. 9, Answers will vary. 3.
6, Answers will vary. 4. 9, Answers will vary.

Page 16
1. 54 marbles; 2. 32 cards; 3. 45 times; 4. 30
miles; 5. 28 skaters; 6. 48 bandages

Page 17
1. 81 boxes; 2. 56 students; 3. 42 picture; 4. 72
cards; 5. 14 pages; 6. 40 marbles

Page 18
1. 6 goldfish; 2. 4 bracelets; 3. 4 points; 4. 5
trophies; 5. 3 buttons; 6. 7 pages

Page 19
1. 9 stamps; 2. 8 rocks; 3. 9 necklaces; 4. 3 miles;
5. 7 crayons; 6. 9 minutes

Page 20
1. 9, 6, 10, 3; 2. 7, 9, 7, 4; 3. 9, 3, 9, 4; 4. 8, 8, 9, 10;
5. 7, 4, 5, 7; 6. 6, 6, 9; 7. 42, 45, 28; 8. 80, 7, 9; 9.
3, 30, 30; 10. 2, 49, 8

Page 21

1.

Rule: × 2	
2	14
3	6
4	8
5	10
6	12
7	14
8	16

2.

Rule: ÷ 3	
12	4
21	7
30	10
15	5
60	20
24	8
9	3

3.

Rule: × 5	
2	10
3	15
4	20
5	25
6	30
7	35
8	40

4.

Rule: ÷ 4	
2	10
3	8
4	1
5	11
6	9
7	7
8	4

5. × 4; 6. ÷ 5

Page 22
1. 2 × 4 = 8, 4 × 2 = 8; 2. 2 × 6 = 12, 6 × 2 = 12;
3. 3 × 4 = 12, 4 × 3 = 12; 4. 3 × 5 = 15, 5 × 3 = 15;
5. 2 × 5 = 10, 5 × 2 = 10; 6. 4 × 5 = 20, 5 × 4 = 20;
7. 24; 8. 30; 9. 14; 10. 16; 11. 24; 12. 18; 13. 8; 14. 5; 15.
2; 16. 3; 17. 3; 18. 9

Page 23
1. (2 × 6) × 1 = 12, 2 × (6 × 1) = 12; 2. (9 × 10) × 1 =
90, 9 × (10 × 1) = 90; 3. (7 × 4) × 3 = 84, 7 × (4 ×
3) = 84; 4. (8 × 3) × 2 = 48, 8 × (3 × 2) = 48;
5. (10 × 5) × 4 = 200, 10 × (5 × 4) = 200;
6. (3 × 4) × 2 = 24, 3 × (4 × 2) = 24;
7. (4 × 2) × 5 = 40, 4 × (2 × 5) = 40;
8. (2 × 10) × 3 = 60, 2 × (10 × 3) = 60

Page 24
1. 56; 2. 51; 3. 110; 4. 72; 5. 78; 6. 84

Page 25
1. 6; 2. 1; 3. 5; 4. 8; 5. 7; 6. 9; 7. 10; 8. 2; 9. 4; 10. 3;
A SWIFTWALKER

Answer Key

Page 26
1. 30, 49, 21, 32; 2. 45, 18, 42, 45; 3. 81, 24, 21, 36; 4. 56, 54, 36, 64; 5. 48, 60, 15, 18, 55, 28, 24; 6. 6, 35, 18, 24, 32, 10, 27; 7. 16, 9, 45, 12, 42, 30, 48; 8. 36, 63, 56, 40, 36, 32, 49; 9. 25, 28, 72, 14; 10. 21, 54, 70, 36

Page 27
1. 3, 2; 2. 4, 3; 3. 3, 5; 4. 2, 5; 5. 8, 2; 6. 5, 4; 7. 4, 6; 8. 7, 4; 9. 4, 9; 10. 2, 8; 11. 8, 6; 12. 6, 9; 13. 8; 14. 7; 15. 9; 16. 8; 17. 7; 18. 7; 19. 4; 20. 5; 21. 9; 22. 8; 23. 8; 24. 4; 25. Answers will vary.

Page 28
1. 27, 27, 3, 9; 2. 28, 28, 4, 7; 3. 16, 16, 2, 8; 4. 30, 30, 5, 6; 5. 54, 54, 6, 9; 6. 56, 56, 8, 7

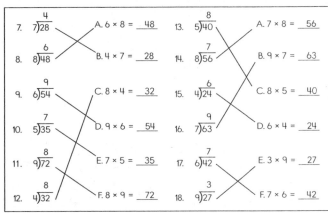

Page 29
1. 7 × 8 = 56, 8 × 7 = 56, 56 ÷ 8 = 7, 56 ÷ 7 = 8; 2. 6 × 7 = 42, 7 × 6 = 42, 42 ÷ 7 = 6, 42 ÷ 6 = 7; 3. 4 × 5 = 20, 5 × 4 = 20, 20 ÷ 5 = 4, 20 ÷ 4 = 5; 4. 9 × 8 = 72, 8 × 9 = 72, 72 ÷ 9 = 8, 72 ÷ 8 = 9; 5. 9 × 7 = 63, 7 × 9 = 63, 63 ÷ 7 = 9, 63 ÷ 9 = 7; 6. 9 × 6 = 54, 6 × 9 = 54, 54 ÷ 6 = 9, 54 ÷ 9 = 6; 7. 6 × 8 = 48, 8 × 6 = 48, 48 ÷ 6 = 8, 48 ÷ 8 = 6; 8. 8 × 4 = 32, 4 × 8 = 32, 32 ÷ 4 = 8, 32 ÷ 8 = 4; 9. 4 × 9 = 36, 9 × 4 = 36, 36 ÷ 9 = 4, 36 ÷ 4 = 9; 10. 7 × 7 = 49, 49 ÷ 7 = 7; 11. 8 × 8 = 64, 64 ÷ 8 = 8; 12. 9 × 9 = 81, 81 ÷ 9 = 9

Page 30
1. Yes. The total of the two items is $3.48. 2. Yes, he will get $1.53 in change. 3. No, he does not. Six quarters equals $1.50. He needs $1.99 for a pineapple. 4. Answers will vary.

Page 31
1. 10 sundaes; 2. 8 bones; 3. 14 more apples; 4. 21 games; 5. 4 walnuts; 6. 3 cookies each, 3 left over

Page 32
Answers will vary.

Page 33

×	1	2	3	4	5	6	7	8	9
1	1	2	3	4	5	6	7	8	9
2	2	4	6	8	10	12	14	16	18
3	3	6	9	12	15	18	21	24	27
4	4	8	12	16	20	24	28	32	36
5	5	10	15	20	25	30	35	40	45
6	6	12	18	24	30	36	42	48	54
7	7	14	21	28	35	42	49	56	63
8	8	16	24	32	40	48	56	64	72
9	9	18	27	36	45	54	63	72	81

1. itself; 2. The numbers are all even; the numbers increase by 2 each time. 3. Answers will vary but may include all numbers ending in either a 5 or a 0. 4. 9; 5. 12

Page 34
1. 40; 2. 60; 3. 60; 4. 90; 5. 70; 6. 30; 7. 30; 8. 40; 9. 20; 10. 40; 11. 300; 12. 990; 13. 460; 14. 430; 15. 690; 16. 920; 17. 780; 18. 380; 19. 250; 20. 720; 21. about 40 nuts; 22. about 20 more stamps

Page 35
1. $700; 2. $100; 3. $600; 4. $300; 5. $700; 6. $900; 7. $700; 8. $500; 9. $900

Page 36
1. 70; 2. 60; 3. 10; 4. 60; 5. 80; 6. 20; 7. 50; 8. 30; 9. 300; 10. 900; 11. 600; 12. 400; 13. 800; 14. 700; 15. 700; 16. 200; 17. about 10 more points; 18. about 90 seashells; 19. about 100 or 160 cards left; 20. about 800 or 820 labels

Page 37
1. 5 + 9 = 14, 9 + 5 = 14, 14 − 9 = 5, 14 − 5 = 9; 2. 8 + 7 = 15, 7 + 8 = 15, 15 − 8 = 7, 15 − 7 = 8; 3. 4 + 9 = 13, 9 + 4 = 13, 13 − 9 = 4, 13 − 4 = 9; 4. 4 + 7 = 11, 7 + 4 = 11, 11 − 7 = 4, 11 − 4 = 7; 5. 7 + 9 = 16, 9 + 7 = 16, 16 − 9 = 7, 16 − 7 = 9;

Answer Key

6. 6 + 7 = 13, 7 + 6 = 13, 13 – 7 = 6, 13 – 6 = 7;
7. 23 + 43 = 66, 43 + 23 = 66, 66 – 23 = 43, 66
– 43 = 23; 8. 52 + 33 = 85, 33 + 52 = 85, 85 – 52
= 33, 85 – 33 = 52; 9. 39 + 71 = 110, 71 + 39 = 110,
110 – 71 = 39, 110 – 39 = 71; 10–12. Answers will
vary. 13. 6

Page 38
1. 49, 59, 98, 89, 96, 49; 2. 73, 87, 27, 68, 95, 57;
3. 54, 40, 22, 65, 61, 15; 4. 26, 20, 24, 23, 51, 50;
5. 885, 778, 988, 998, 527; 6. 594, 986, 969, 789,
919; 7. 431, 213, 225, 236, 223; 8. 553, 322, 812, 121,
205

Page 39
1. 51, 92, 81, 86, 64, 90; 2. 94, 130, 92, 92, 103, 102;
3. 19, 79, 19, 26, 16, 49; 4. 19, 58, 14, 59, 28, 32;
5. 940, 610, 1,091, 1,311, 420; 6. 611, 613, 617, 1,211,
1,059; 7. 699, 269, 469, 429, 257; 8. 187, 292, 739,
289, 228

Page 40
1. 80, 70, 40, 90, 30; 2. 60, 100, 20, 50, 30; 3. 40,
420, 60, 240, 810; 4. 400, 120, 560, 300, 200

Page 41

×	10	20	30	40	50	60	70	80	90
1	10	20	30	40	50	60	70	80	90
2	20	40	60	80	100	120	140	160	180
3	30	60	90	120	150	180	210	240	270
4	40	80	120	160	200	240	280	320	360
5	50	100	150	200	250	300	350	400	450
6	60	120	180	240	300	360	420	480	540
7	70	140	210	280	350	420	490	560	630
8	80	160	240	320	400	480	560	640	720
9	90	180	270	360	450	540	630	720	810

Answers will vary.

Page 42
1. ⊠; 2. $\frac{1}{4}$; 3. ⊠; 4. $\frac{1}{3}$; 5. $\frac{1}{6}$; 6. ⊗; 7. Wyatt
is correct because the shape is not divided into
three equal pieces. 8. Yes, he did. While the
shapes are different, they are both divided into
four equal pieces, and both have three of the
four sections shaded.

Page 43
1. $\frac{1}{6}$; 2. $\frac{3}{8}$; 3. $\frac{1}{2}$; 4. $\frac{5}{8}$; 5. $\frac{10}{16}$; 6. $\frac{7}{12}$

Page 44
1. $\frac{3}{6}$ or $\frac{1}{2}$; 2. $\frac{5}{8}$; 3. $\frac{4}{4}$ or 1; 4. $\frac{4}{8}$ or $\frac{1}{2}$; 5. $\frac{11}{32}$;
6. $\frac{6}{12}$ or $\frac{1}{2}$

Page 45
1. $\frac{4}{6}$ or $\frac{2}{3}$; 2. $\frac{1}{3}$; 3. $\frac{1}{4}$; 4. $\frac{1}{4}$; 5. $\frac{1}{3}$; 6. $\frac{2}{4}$ or $\frac{1}{2}$; 7.
$\frac{3}{6}$ or $\frac{1}{2}$; 8. $\frac{3}{8}$; 9. $\frac{2}{4}$ or $\frac{1}{2}$; 10. $\frac{1}{2}$; 11. $\frac{1}{4}$; 12. $\frac{2}{4}$ or
$\frac{1}{2}$; 13. $\frac{3}{4}$; 14. $\frac{6}{12}$ or $\frac{1}{2}$; 15. $\frac{5}{15}$ or $\frac{1}{3}$

Page 46
1. $\frac{13}{15}$; 2. $\frac{2}{10}$ or $\frac{1}{5}$; 3. $\frac{5}{7}$; 4. $\frac{7}{8}$; 5. $\frac{24}{48}$ or $\frac{1}{2}$; 6. $\frac{3}{8}$

Page 47
1. $\frac{1}{2}$; 2. $\frac{1}{4}$; 3. $\frac{2}{4}$ or $\frac{1}{2}$; 4. $\frac{1}{4}$; 5. $\frac{3}{8}$; 6. $\frac{1}{8}$ or $\frac{2}{4}$;
7. $\frac{3}{8}$; 8. $\frac{4}{8}$, $\frac{2}{4}$ or $\frac{1}{2}$; 9. $\frac{5}{8}$; 10. $\frac{6}{8}$ or $\frac{3}{4}$; 11. $\frac{7}{8}$

Page 48
1. $\frac{1}{2}$; 2. $\frac{1}{3}$; 3. $\frac{2}{3}$; 4. $\frac{1}{6}$; 5. $\frac{2}{6}$ or $\frac{1}{3}$; 6. $\frac{3}{6}$ or $\frac{1}{2}$; 7.
$\frac{4}{6}$ or $\frac{2}{3}$; 8. $\frac{5}{6}$

Page 49

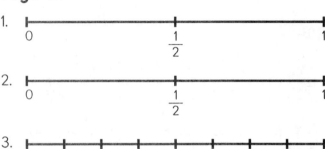

Answer Key

Page 50

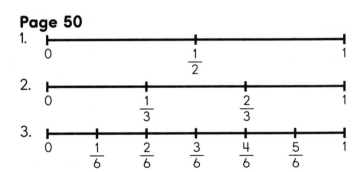

Page 51

1. $\frac{1}{6}$, $\frac{2}{3}$; 2. $\frac{3}{6}$, $\frac{4}{6}$, $\frac{5}{6}$; 3. $\frac{3}{8}$, $\frac{4}{8}$, $\frac{8}{8}$; 4. $\frac{1}{3}$, $\frac{1}{2}$, $\frac{2}{3}$;

5. (number line: 0, $\frac{1}{8}$, $\frac{2}{8}$ '$\frac{1}{4}$, $\frac{3}{8}$, $\frac{4}{8}$ '$\frac{2}{4}$, $\frac{5}{8}$, $\frac{6}{8}$ '$\frac{3}{4}$, $\frac{7}{8}$, 1)

6. (number line: 0, $\frac{1}{6}$, $\frac{2}{6}$,$\frac{1}{3}$, $\frac{3}{6}$, $\frac{4}{6}$,$\frac{2}{3}$, $\frac{5}{6}$)

7. Answers will vary.

Page 52

1. 5; 2. $\frac{2}{4}$, $\frac{3}{6}$, $\frac{4}{8}$; 3. $\frac{2}{6}$; 4. $\frac{3}{6}$; 5. $\frac{3}{4}$; 6. $\frac{6}{8}$;

7. $\frac{2}{6}$; 8. $\frac{1}{1}$, $\frac{2}{2}$, $\frac{3}{3}$, $\frac{4}{4}$, $\frac{5}{5}$, $\frac{6}{6}$, $\frac{7}{7}$, $\frac{8}{8}$

Page 53

1. $\frac{1}{3}$ = $\frac{2}{4}$; 2. $\frac{1}{4}$ = $\frac{2}{8}$; 3. $\frac{1}{2}$ = $\frac{3}{6}$; 4. $\frac{3}{4}$ = $\frac{6}{8}$;

5. $\frac{2}{2}$ = $\frac{1}{1}$ or 1; 6. $\frac{3}{7}$ = $\frac{6}{14}$; 7. $\frac{1}{5}$ = $\frac{2}{10}$;

8. $\frac{1}{6}$ = $\frac{2}{12}$; 9. $\frac{8}{8}$ = $\frac{1}{1}$ or 1; 10. $\frac{2}{3}$ = $\frac{6}{9}$;

11. $\frac{2}{4}$ = $\frac{8}{16}$; 12. $\frac{1}{4}$ = $\frac{3}{12}$

Page 54

1. $\frac{2}{8}$ or $\frac{1}{4}$; 2. $\frac{4}{6}$ or $\frac{2}{3}$; 3. $\frac{2}{4}$ or $\frac{1}{2}$; 4. $\frac{4}{12}$ or $\frac{1}{3}$;

5. $\frac{12}{32}$ or $\frac{3}{8}$; 6. $\frac{1}{2}$ or $\frac{2}{4}$ = $\frac{4}{8}$; 7. $\frac{2}{3}$ or $\frac{4}{6}$ = $\frac{8}{12}$;

8. $\frac{2}{3}$ = $\frac{2}{6}$; 9. $\frac{1}{6}$, $\frac{5}{6}$ (circled); 10. $\frac{2}{6}$, $\frac{4}{6}$ (circled);

11. $\frac{3}{6}$, $\frac{3}{6}$; 12. $\frac{4}{6}$ (circled), $\frac{2}{6}$; 13. $\frac{5}{6}$ (circled), $\frac{1}{6}$;

14. $\frac{6}{6}$ (circled), 0

Page 55

1. 2; 2. 2; 3. 4; 4. 8; 5. 4; 6. 2; 7. 2; 8. 2, 6, 4

Page 56

1. The fractions $\frac{2}{4}$ and $\frac{1}{2}$ are equivalent because they both fall on the same spot on the number line.

2. (number line: 0, $\frac{1}{6}$, $\frac{2}{6}$,$\frac{1}{3}$, $\frac{3}{6}$, $\frac{4}{6}$,$\frac{2}{3}$, $\frac{5}{6}$, 1)

3. $\frac{1}{4}$ = $\frac{2}{8}$, $\frac{2}{4}$ = $\frac{4}{8}$, $\frac{3}{4}$ = $\frac{6}{8}$; 4. Answers will vary but may include $\frac{2}{2}$, $\frac{3}{3}$, $\frac{4}{4}$, $\frac{5}{5}$, $\frac{6}{6}$, $\frac{7}{7}$, or $\frac{8}{8}$. They are equivalent because on a number line they all fall on the same spot.

5. They are not equivalent because $\frac{5}{8}$ is greater than $\frac{1}{2}$. 6. Answers will vary but may include two or more fractions that equal the same amount, Answers will vary.

Page 57

1. 2, 2; 2. 2, 10; 3. 2, 2; 4. 4, 8; 5. 3, 6; 6. 3, 9; 7. 4, 12; 8. 3, 15; 9. 4, 28; 10. 7, 28; 11. 5, 40; 12. 4, 20

Page 58

1. $\frac{12}{3}$; 2. $\frac{4}{2}$; 3. $\frac{12}{6}$; 4. $\frac{20}{4}$; 5. $\frac{10}{2}$; 6. $\frac{24}{6}$; 7. $\frac{3}{1}$;

8. $\frac{4}{1}$; 9. $\frac{2}{1}$; 10–15. Answers will vary.

Page 59

1. 4; 2. 5; 3. 4; 4. 6; 5. 2; 6. 5; 7. 7; 8. 7; 9. 8; 10. 9; 11. 3; 12. 5; 13. 11; 14. 10; 15. 10; 16. 6

Page 60

1. $\frac{2}{2}$; 2. $\frac{4}{4}$; 3. $\frac{8}{8}$; 4. $\frac{3}{3}$; 5. $\frac{6}{6}$; 6. Answers will vary.

7.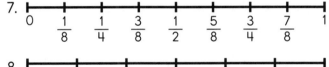

8.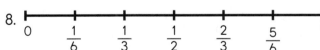

Answer Key

Page 61

1. $\dfrac{1}{3} < \dfrac{2}{3}$; 2. $\dfrac{2}{4} = \dfrac{4}{8}$; 3. $\dfrac{3}{8} < \dfrac{1}{2}$; 4. $\dfrac{1}{3} = \dfrac{2}{6}$;

5. $\dfrac{3}{4} > \dfrac{2}{4}$; 6. $\dfrac{1}{2} < \dfrac{3}{4}$

Page 62

1. <; 2. <; 3. >; 4. <; 5. >; 6. > 7. If the denominators are the same, the fraction with the smaller numerator is <u>smaller</u>. 8. >; 9. <; 10. <; 11. <; 12. >; 13. >; 14. If the numerators are the same, the fraction with the smaller denominator is <u>greater</u>.

Page 63

1. 12:18; 2. 6:16; 3. 8:33; 4. 11:18

5.   6.   7.   8.

Page 64

1. 4:58; 2. 6:22; 3. 3:08; 4. 10:20; 5. 1:35; 6. 7:53; 7. 6:03; 8. 12:26; 9. 4:49

Page 65

Page 66

1. The times that shows start and end at; 2. 4 hours; 3. 2 hours; 4. 45 minutes; 5. 2 hours; 6. 1 hour 30 minutes

Page 67

1. 8:00, 7:40, 11:35, 9:05; 2. 1:38, 12:50, 7:00, 2:35; 3. 10:45, 2:30, 3:00, 12:00; 4. 12:25, 3:25, 9:31, 4:12

Page 68

1. 37 minutes; 2. 9:00 pm; 3. 7 minutes; 4. 8:47 pm; 5. 1 hour, 21 minutes; 6. 3 hours

Page 69

1. 7:55 am; 2. 4:40 pm; 3. 3:24 pm; 4. 5:43 pm; 5. 8:21 pm; 6. 11 hours

Page 70

1. 7:05 am; 2. 7:40 am; 3. 8:25 am; 4. 8:45 am; 5. 3:35 pm; 6. 3:55 pm; 7. 5:10 pm; 8. 5:45 pm

Page 71

1. A. L; 2. B. mL; 3. B. mL; 4. A. L; 5. B. mL; 6. 15 L; 7. 21 L; 8. 645 mL; 9. 2 L

Page 72

1. A. g; 2. B. kg; 3. B. kg; 4. A. g; 5. A. g; 6. 4 apples; 7. 8 kg; 8. 12 kg; 9. baseball, Answers will vary.

Page 73

1. 65 cm; 2. food A, food D; 3. 55 cm; 4. 45 cm; 5. food B, food E; 6. 35 cm

Page 74

1. grade 4; 2. grade 5; 3. 1,860 pounds; 4. 300 pounds; 5. grade 6; 6. 60 pounds; 7. grade 6; 8. 780 pounds

Page 75

1. strawberry; 2. grape and orange; 3. apple; 4. cherry; 5. Madison Elementary; 6. 14 volunteers; 7. 6 more; 8. Madison Elementary

Page 76

1. $2\dfrac{1}{2}$ in; 2. $2\dfrac{3}{4}$ in; 3. 1 in; 4. $5\dfrac{1}{4}$ in; 5. 3 in; 6. $3\dfrac{1}{2}$ in; 7. $2\dfrac{1}{4}$ in; 8. 4 in; 9. $3\dfrac{1}{2}$ in; 10. $1\dfrac{3}{4}$ in.

Answer Key

Page 77

1. 1 in; 2. $\frac{1}{2}$ in; 3. 1 $\frac{1}{4}$ in; 4. $\frac{1}{4}$ in; 5. $\frac{1}{4}$ in; 6. 1 in; 7. 1 in; 8. 1 $\frac{1}{4}$ in; 9. $\frac{1}{2}$ in; 10. $\frac{1}{2}$ in. and 1 in; 11. $\frac{3}{4}$ in; 12. 2 more; 13. 9

Page 78

1. 3 $\frac{1}{2}$; 2. 2; 3. 3; 4. 2 $\frac{3}{4}$; 5. 2; 6. 2 $\frac{3}{4}$

Page 79

1. 8; 2. 10; 3. 10; 4. 8; 5. 16; 6. 7; 7. 10; 8. 11; 9. 22

Page 80

1. 24 sq. units; 2. 40 sq. units; 3. 40 sq. units; 4. 30 sq. units; 5. 51 sq. units; 6. 24 sq. units;

7. 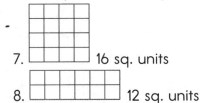 16 sq. units

8. 12 sq. units

9. 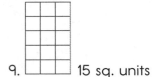 15 sq. units

Page 81

1. 72; 2. 24; 3. 50; 4. 18; 5. 16; 6. 80; 7. Answers will vary.

Page 82

1. 91 sq. ft. 2. 100 sq. m; 3. 136 sq. ft. 4. 72 sq. in. 5. 51 sq. ft. 6. 18 sq. in.

Page 83

1. 24; 2. 10; 3. 24; 4. 16; 5. 21; 6. 32

Page 84

1. 15 sq. ft., 16 ft. 2. 6 sq. ft., 10 ft. 3. 6 sq. ft., 10 ft. 4. 20 sq. ft., 18 ft. 5. 16 sq. ft. 6. 2 feet larger

Page 85

1. quadrilateral; 2. triangle; 3. triangle; 4. pentagon; 5. quadrilateral; 6. triangle; 7. pentagon; 8. pentagon; 9. quadrilateral; 10. triangle; 11. quadrilateral; 12. pentagon

Page 86

1. rectangle, It has four sides and two sets of parallel sides. 2. octagon, It has eight sides. 3. pentagon, It has five sides. 4. square, It has four equal sides. 5. triangle, It has three sides. 6. hexagon, It has six sides.

Page 87

1. square, rectangle, trapezoid, rhombus; 2. square; 3. triangle; 4. circle; 5. pentagon; 6. hexagon; 7. octagon; 8. square, rectangle, trapezoid, hexagon, rhombus, octagon; 9. Answers will vary but may include that a rhombus has two sets of parallel lines; a trapezoid has one set or that all sides in a rhombus are equal.

Page 88

1. rhombus; 2. rectangle; 3. quadrilateral; 4. quadrilateral; 5. square; 6. parallelogram; 7. rectangle; 8. parallelogram; 9. quadrilateral; 10. square; 11. They are all quadrilaterals.

12-15. Check students' drawings.

Page 89

1. A. fourths; B. ; C. fourths; D. ;

2. A. ; B. fourths; C. sixths; D.

3. A. or ; B. ; C. ; D. ;

4. A. ; B. ; C. or ; D.

Page 90

1-4. Answers will vary.

96